KEEPER OF LOST LOVES

A SERENITY FALLS COZY ROMANCE

IRIS APPLEWOOD

Enchanted Owl

Also by Iris Applewood

Serenity Falls

Fragrance of Forgotten Truths: A Serenity Falls Cozy Mystery

Enchanted Owl

enchantedowlpublishing.com

Book cover by Angie Andriot

First edition 2024

To my beloved family, who have been the warm hearth against every blizzard of my creative and professional pursuits.

CONTENTS

Chapter One

COOKIE CRUSADE

Fireside Manor Bed and Breakfast's kitchen was a battlefield, and I was its lone warrior, armed with a whisk and a spatula. Flour dusted every surface like the aftermath of a blizzard, and the sweet aroma of baking cookies filled the air. My hair, once neatly tied back, now sported rebellious strands that I brushed away with flour-dusted fingers.

I'd decided, in what I now realized was a moment of sheer madness, to bake enough cookies for the entire town festival. 'Community spirit,' they called it. I called it a test of sanity.

This cookie crusade, though cloaked in the guise of town camaraderie, had a secondary, more utilitarian aim. Each cinnamon-scented bite was, in fact, a subtle advertisement. A delicious nudge for folks to chat about Fireside Manor. Maybe even check in for a night or two.

Yet, this pragmatic angle didn't diminish the genuine warmth of the gesture, right? It wasn't as though my bed and breakfast was just a pit stop for travelers; it was a living scrapbook. Each room was lovingly designed to hold stories of joy, laughter, and heartfelt sighs from guests. My story? Well, that was more like an aside, scribbled in the margins. But if my cookies could entice more people to add their tales to this scrapbook, then all this floury madness would be worth it.

I glanced at the clock. "Get it together, Clara. Only an hour left."

Swinging open the oven door to juggle another batch of cookies, I was greeted with a gust of hot air that felt almost like a hug. As always, I toyed with the idea of just parking myself in front of the oven, holding out my sweater so the warm air billowed beneath.

Or maybe just curl up inside. Cozy, warm, and with the added bonus of being surrounded by cookies. Tempting, but it might raise a few eyebrows.

Then my phone buzzed in my pocket. Potential guest or another telemarketer? I wiped my floury hands on my apron and fished out the phone, hoping for the former. Glancing at the screen, I saw Jenna's name. Must be news from the festival front.

I put the phone on speaker so I could move the finished cookies to a cooling rack. This batch of soft and chewy spice cookies should melt even the frostiest of hearts.

"Clara, where are you?" Jenna's voice buzzed with excitement. "The artists are all set up, and the crowds are already swarming."

Peering at my still-dirty mixer on the granite countertop, I responded, half-distracted. "Just wrestling the last batch of cookies. They've been fussier than a cat in a room full of rocking chairs."

Jenna's laughter rang through. "It's a Christmas festival, Clara, not a bake-off showdown. Remember to have fun, not just add to your stress."

"I know, I know." I tried not to laugh while transferring cookies to the cooling rack. "But these aren't just cookies; they're Fireside Manor's charming little diplomats." I tried to suppress a sigh. "You'd think after two years I'd have this thing down."

"You should be proud of all you've accomplished in that time. I still remember bringing in my artwork, finding you amidst a sea of renovation plans. You've really transformed the place since then."

"Yeah, it's been quite the journey." I put the last batch of cookies in the oven. "Remember how this place looked when I first bought it? More like a scene from a horror movie than a cozy B&B."

Jenna chuckled. "I do. But you saw something in it, a potential that no one else did. It's like you were meant to find it."

I gazed lovingly at my kitchen. The cheerful butter-yellow walls now held memories of laughter and shared secrets. Pots and pans, each with their own story, hung in an orderly chaos above the island, witnesses to countless meals and experiments. In this kitchen, warmth and comfort were indeed served in generous portions, the very air infused with a sense of belonging. "Feels like a whirlwind romance, doesn't it? Finding this place, secluded, forgotten, and just begging for a new life."

"Just like you were," said Jenna.

I resisted the urge to stuff all the cookies in my mouth to suppress my memory of that fateful day when my life unraveled. It was during one of my lower moments, scrolling through real estate listings, that I stumbled upon it—a gorgeous, abandoned mansion nestled in the woods on the outskirts of Serenity Falls, the humble hamlet I now call home. It was nothing like the bustling city I grew up in. The estate, brimming with hidden potential and forgotten charm, whispered to me like a secret waiting to be told. On a whim, I made the decision that would redefine my future—I used the last of my savings to scrape together a down payment.

And despite the struggles to get the B&B off the ground, I regretted nothing. "And now, despite every challenge, it's become more than just a business. It's like a piece of my soul."

Jenna's warm affirmation came through. "And a charming piece at that. But hey, promise me you'll take a moment to enjoy the festival too, okay? It's not all about the business hustle."

"Of course. I'll mingle and flash my 'hostess of the year' smile." I actually planned to drop off the cookies and bolt. "But I've got to rush back by four. Our mystery guest is checking in today–the one who's booked solo, all month to Christmas Eve. I wonder what his story is."

"I bet he's one of those city types, seeking a quaint village holiday. Perhaps even looking for his own real-life Hallmark moment." Jenna's voice brimmed so heavily with playful suggestion, I could practically hear her eyebrows waggle.

I held back a sigh. My romance-loving friend was always trying to hook me up with someone. As though two years were long enough to get over... well, let's not go there. It was hardly Jenna's fault. She was still in her twenties; they bounced back so quickly at that age. Not that Jenna had much to bounce back from. Pickings were slim in a small town. And even slimmer when you only dated other women.

"Maybe he's just dodging a house full of overzealous relatives," I replied, trying to maneuver the subject away from my love life.

"Or he's a charming serial killer looking for a festive hideout."

"Serial killer or not, his stay is a Christmas gift to the Manor's finances." My tone was joking, but seriously—I was about to the point where I'd help him hide the bodies, as long as he paid for his stay up front. Guests had been playing a tad hard-to-get with Fireside Manor.

I glared at the letter from the bank, sitting on my counter. Okay, a lot hard-to-get. Despite its charm and my efforts, my objectively fantastic B&B seemed to be the wallflower of the village accommodations dance.

Jenna's voice was playful, yet sincere. "Just promise me you'll stay on the safe side of adventurous, okay? We need our Clara in one piece for the New Year!"

"Don't worry," I said. "I've got my trusty rolling pin. It's good for more than just baking, you know."

The oven timer dinged, a sound that was becoming the sound-track of my afternoon. I promised Jenna I'd be there soon and hung up, pulling out the last tray of perfectly browned cookies. "Nailed it," I said, giving myself a high-five because, well, someone had to.

I arranged the cookies meticulously in wicker baskets, each layer nestled between festive napkins that I had craftily stamped with Fireside Manor's logo—a subtle yet charming little inn with a smoking chimney that was sure to etch the B&B into people's minds. With each bite, they'd think of cozy rooms, crackling fireplaces, and the possibility of more delicious indulgences awaiting them here.

The cookies looked almost too good to eat, each a miniature billboard for my labor of love. Almost. Spotting one that got a bit too brown around the edges, I plucked it from the basket. "Quality control," I reasoned aloud, giving the cookie a scrutinizing look before taking a bite.

The rich, spiced flavor was a small victory, but the real triumph, I thought, was in the packaging. Inscribed on each napkin was my inn's catchy motto—Fireside Manor Bed and Breakfast: Where Warmth Meets Wonder.

Taking another bite, I felt a surge of determination mingled with sweet satisfaction. If the tantalizing lure of fresh-baked treats didn't start a buzz, I'd have to think of something even more inventive. I wasn't about to let Fireside Manor sink into obscurity. Especially with the bank breathing down my neck.

With the baskets filled to the brim, I surveyed the kitchen. My apron, a canvas of flour, sugar, and cinnamon, hung from my neck like a badge of honor. There was a time I would have fretted about appearances, changed into a pristine apron before stepping out. But those days were gone. Why bother with a clean apron when life, much like love, was bound to splatter you with a new mess, anyway?

I shrugged into my coat, pulling it over the colorful mess. Hat snugly in place, I gave the kitchen one final, lingering glance. The pulsing heart of Fireside Manor. With this heartfelt tableau etched in my mind, I stepped out, closing the door on a room that was a repository of both culinary delights and unvoiced yearnings.

The festival awaited, with its twinkling lights and merry chatter, and I, the Cookie Queen of Serenity Falls, was about to make my grand, unapologetically floury entrance.

CHAPTER TWO

MAGIC KISSES

S tepping into the town square felt akin to trespassing on a film set—one where the director's Christmas Charm obsession might be bordering on a clinical condition. Snowflakes descended like—

Whoosh! There I went, my foot finding the slickest patch of ice this side of the North Pole, transforming my walk into a desperate flail for survival. My arms went into full windmill mode as I made a heroic attempt to save both my dignity and a basket of cookies from a frosty demise. By some stroke of slapstick luck, I remained upright, clutching the basket like it was the Holy Grail.

Exhaling, I scanned the area for any witnesses to my impromptu performance on ice. Thankfully, it seemed my audience was limited to one highly amused pigeon, perched like a fluffy judge on its snowy bench.

Anyway, where were we?

Right. Snowflakes descended like an overly choreographed ballet, dusting Serenity Falls in a layer of snow so picturesque, it was almost offensive. You'd think after two years of witnessing this annual spectacle, the novelty would wear off. But no, here I was, still gazing with the wonder of a child—a child who knew the snow meant extra shoveling.

And that sometimes, the line between a winter wonderland and an ice rink is just one slippery step away.

The snow-dusted cobblestones and rooftops looked suspiciously perfect, each flake glistening under the weak afternoon sun as if they were part of a carefully curated winter exhibit. The unlit strings of twinkling lights hung between lampposts added a touch of anticipation, hinting at the fleeting romances they would bring come evening.

The air rang with laughter and choral music, the kind that's about joy and love and all that jazz. The local choir was giving it their all, visible puffs of their enthusiasm escaping into the cold air. Kids were running around, their energy levels unaffected by the cold, leaving behind a chaos of footprints.

Clutching my basket of cookies, which felt like my shield against all this festivity, I steeled myself. Time to spread some cookie-induced cheer and maybe, just maybe, dodge any mistletoe encounters. After all, the only thing more fleeting than holiday romance was a New Year's resolution.

As I plunged headfirst into the cheerful crowds, the mingling scents of mulled wine, roasted chestnuts, and pine flooded my nose. It was like the village had its own brand of perfume: Eau de Christmas Overload. I wove past stalls with barely a glance, where vendors displayed goods that screamed, "buy me for someone you love"—a concept I found both endearing and nauseating.

Navigating through a sea of red and green sweaters, I arrived at the dessert table, a cornucopia of festive confectioneries that could send a dentist into despair. I wedged my basket of cookies between a tower of mince pies and a battalion of gingerbread men. "Make room for the new recruits," I announced to the desserts, arranging my cookies with a flourish that was more for my own amusement than anyone else's.

As I stepped back to admire my handiwork, a tap on my shoulder startled me. Turning around, I came face to face with Ms. Doris Fletcher, Serenity Falls's unofficial historian and chief busybody. She had a way of appearing out of thin air at the most inconvenient times, and today was no exception. The woman stood there, her presence as commanding as her colorful outfit, ready to dish out her blend of advice with the same flair as she dressed.

"Clara, dear, those cookies look divine." Doris was clad in a vibrant, patterned dress that seemed to capture the essence of every festival she had ever attended—a patchwork of history in fabric form. Over her dress, she wore a cardigan the color of ripe cranberries, adorned with an assortment of brooches that sparkled under the festival lights. On her head sat a jaunty hat, festooned with a band of artificial holly that nodded as she spoke, adding a whimsical touch to her already... ahem... striking ensemble.

"Thank you, Doris." I flashed a practiced smile.

"And how are you keeping? Still warding off those young bachelors with a broom?" Her eyes, bright and keen, sparkled with mirth behind round spectacles that seemed to magnify not just her vision but her ability to see into the very heart of Serenity Falls's happenings. Doris, having never had children of her own, appeared to find purpose in adopting the entire town, anointing herself as Serenity Falls's unofficial, yet universally acknowledged, resident grandmother—a very, very involved grandmother.

"Oh, you know me, Doris. I find my cookies are a more effective deterrent. Less chance of a lawsuit."

She chuckled, her laughter carrying a warmth that contradicted the cold nipping at our noses. "Always so witty. But mark my words, dear, love will find you when you least expect it."

I raised an eyebrow, a smile tugging at my lips. "I'll believe it when I see it. For now, I'm more interested in these cookies finding their way into everyone's stomachs."

Doris gave me a knowing look, as if she had already plotted the entire course of my love life. Her attention then drifted to the Fireside Manor napkins nestled under the cookies. She picked one up, examining it with an air of discovery. "Ah, I see," she murmured, her eyes flicking back to mine. "These cookies are practically a billboard for your B&B!"

I maintained a polite smile, resisting the urge to smooth out the napkin she had just disturbed. "Well, Doris, we do what we can."

Doris traced the embossed logo on the napkin, her expression softening. "It's nice to see the old manor getting a new life."

I nodded, but Doris, despite her words, had never once actually crossed the threshold of Fireside Manor. I wondered if it was just a lack of interest or something more. "You know, Doris, you should come by and see it for yourself one of these days. I'd love to give you a tour, show you the transformations we've made."

Doris placed the napkin back down, aligning it along the edge of the table with precise care. "Oh, that's very kind of you, dear." Her tone was polite yet noncommittal. "But you know, with my knee acting up and all, it's difficult for me to get around these days. Perhaps another time." There was a finality in her voice that suggested the offer, while appreciated, would remain unaccepted.

"Of course. You're welcome anytime." I smiled. "Just let me know, and I'll make sure everything is comfortable for you."

As I watched her nod appreciatively, a flicker of frustration ignited within me. Since moving to Serenity Falls, I had been enveloped in a community that was warm and welcoming whenever I ventured into town. Yet, despite this friendliness, it struck me that, other than Jenna, nobody seemed willing to make the extra journey to visit me at Fireside Manor, despite the numerous events I tried to host for the town.

It was as if there was an invisible barrier surrounding the B&B, one that locals hesitated to cross. You'd think the place was haunted. Or cursed.

Doris leaned in closer, her voice dropping to a conspiratorial whisper. "You know, dear, if you really want to catch people's attention, you should hand these cookies out personally. Makes for a better impression than just leaving them on the dessert table."

I bit back a sigh, knowing she meant well. "That's a good idea, Doris. I hadn't thought of that."

Her eyes gleamed with mischief. "And do it under the mistletoe. Adds a bit of festive charm, don't you think? It would be quite the talk of the town!"

Great. Nothing like a bit of enforced romance to spice up the evening. "Oh, Doris, always full of creative suggestions!"

She clapped her hands, delighted. "Wonderful! You'll see. It'll work wonders. And who knows, maybe a bit of that mistletoe magic might work on you, too."

I laughed, a little too forcefully. "I'd prefer to stick to the magic of baking for now. But thanks for the advice."

As Doris finally wandered off, her holly-adorned hat bobbing with each step, I stood there for a moment, pondering her words. The idea of parading around under the mistletoe with my basket of cookies felt like stepping right into one of Doris's schemes—something I would normally avoid at all costs. But as I watched the crowd, their faces alight with holiday cheer, a reluctant thought crept in. Maybe, just maybe, Doris had a point. It could be a clever way to highlight Fireside Manor, especially under the guise of festive fun.

With a sigh that carried more resignation than I cared to admit, I picked up my basket and headed towards the old oak tree... and its mistletoe. "For the B&B," I whispered under my breath, hoping

Doris wouldn't catch sight of me and chalk it up as a victory. It was a good idea, but I'd never tell her that.

There I stood holding a basket of cookies under the old oak tree adorned with mistletoe. The air was filled with the sound of laughter and the soft melody of holiday tunes. As I took a deep breath, savoring the crisp winter air, I felt a tinge of excitement. Or was it nerves? It was as if the festive atmosphere was weaving its magic around me, leaving a feeling both pleasant and mysteriously undefinable. Almost tingly.

Then, as if scripted in a holiday tale, Tom, the village's favorite baker and widowed heartthrob, materialized beside me. With his tousled hair and that disarming smile that sent half the town into daydreams, he could have stepped straight out of a romance novel—the kind you chuckle at more than believe.

"Clara, fancy meeting you here," he said, a playful lilt in his voice as he suggestively snagged a cookie from my basket. His gaze drifted upward to the mistletoe. "Seems we're both victims of festive fate."

I stifled a sigh. "Seems like fate has a sense of humor." Internally, I braced myself. A peck with the village's most eligible bachelor was bound to set tongues wagging, something I preferred to avoid. "Though I'm only in it for the tradition, mind you."

Expecting a simple gesture, I turned my cheek towards Tom, but in a surprising twist, he planted a quick, soft peck on my lips. It was over in a heartbeat, but in the wake of that brief kiss, a flood of foreign emotions washed over me—a poignant blend of nostalgia and sadness, as unexpected as the kiss itself. Alongside this strange emotional invasion, Tom's voice seemed to echo in my mind. *I still think about her every Christmas...*

For a moment, confusion swirled within me, my thoughts as scattered as snowflakes in a gust. I blinked , trying to clear the fog of surprise, and turned to Tom. "Did you just say something?"

Tom met my gaze, his eyebrows knitting together in bewilderment. "No."

Taking a bite of the cookie, he gave me a friendly, if quizzical, smile before starting to walk away. "Take care, Clara. You might want to ease up on the holiday spirits, though," he joked, leaving a trail of warmth and the faint scent of gingerbread in his wake.

His response left me even more baffled. The words and the emotions had felt so real, so immediate. Yet, if they hadn't come from Tom, then where?

My thoughts were interrupted by a familiar, teasing voice. "Hey, Clara, what's this? A cookies and kisses stand?" Jenna, always the spark in any gathering, approached with a playful grin. Her eyes darted towards Tom, who was now engaged in light-hearted banter with a gaggle of female townsfolk. She leaned in conspiratorially. "Or should I be expecting an announcement from you two?" Her eyebrows danced upward.

A chuckle escaped me despite the lingering bewilderment. "Strictly a business endeavor, Jenna." I extended the basket of cookies.

She picked a spice cookie, examining it with an artist's eye before eyeing the mistletoe and then me, her smile brimming with mischief. "What do you say? Tradition is tradition, after all."

As our lips met in a friendly peck, a surge of emotion and thoughts crashed into me again, just as it had with Tom.

I wish I'd told her how I felt before she left...

The clarity and intensity of the longing in the thought jolted me. My heart raced. This was no coincidence. An image of Maggie, who had moved away last year, floated through my mind. The three of us used to do everything together. Was Jenna secretly in love with

Maggie? Had she been hiding this torch all along, right under my nose?

I needed to find out.

"Speaking of traditions, does it feel weird not having Maggie's holiday party this year?" Last year's Christmas party had been my first introduction to the festivities Maggie had been known for. It was a whirlwind of laughter, impromptu karaoke, and the kind of warmth that only the best of friends could create. On Christmas Eve, she'd transformed her living room into a winter wonderland, complete with faux snow and twinkling lights. We'd all ended up having a mock snowball fight, ducking behind sofas and cushions, our laughter echoing into the night. But amidst the playful chaos, there was this moment when Jenna and Maggie's eyes locked, then a shared smile and a look that lingered just a second too long. It was subtle, but now, in retrospect, it seemed like a silent confession.

"Maggie?" Jenna's smile faltered for a split second, a flicker of something unspoken crossing her face. "Oh yeah, those parties were legendary. She's doing well, last I heard."

Busted. Jenna's face was as transparent as a glass window on a sunny day. I nodded, trying to look nonchalant while my mind whirled. A part of me was curious to dig deeper, but another part—a more cautious, less mistletoe-empowered part—suggested I tread lightly. After all, some secrets, like the perfect recipe for a Christmas cookie, are best savored when they unfold naturally.

But one thing was clear: my kisses were magic. That was the only explanation.

The thought was as unsettling as it was absurd. Since when did my lips come with a side of telepathy?

Jenna gave me a concerned smile. "You're looking a bit out of sorts. Everything okay?"

I laughed, my gaze flickering to my basket of cookies. "Perhaps I've sampled too many of my own wares," I joked, trying to mask the whirlwind of thoughts in my head. Was this some bizarre twist of fate? Here I was, Clara Winters, the eternal skeptic of love stories, potentially gifted (or cursed?) with the ability to hear the innermost thoughts of others—through a kiss, no less.

What an odd joke for the universe to play.

Jenna's smile softened. "Well, duty calls. I've got to get back to my booth. Those hand-painted ornaments won't sell themselves!"

"Of course, good luck with the sales." I watched Jenna gracefully weave her way into the crowd. As she disappeared into the throng of festival-goers, my gaze drifted across the square. The blend of familiar faces and holiday spirit painted a comforting backdrop.

That's when I spotted a man standing out amidst the sea of regulars. He was undeniably attractive, with a kind of polished charm that hinted at city living. His features were striking: sharp jawline, dark hair that was perfectly styled yet gave off an effortless vibe, and a build that suggested he was no stranger to a gym. His piercing blue eyes held a look of slight bewilderment. The classic expression of an out-of-towner trying to blend into local festivities.

"Okay, Clara, time for a little experiment," I whispered to myself. Attractive or not, I had no time for that nonsense. This was purely for science. If I was going to test this bizarre new 'gift' of mine, it might as well be with someone who seemed like he could handle a bit of holiday eccentricity without running for the Serenity Falls hills. And it helped that he wasn't from town.

I sauntered over, putting on my most charming front. "Seems you've found the heart of our little celebration." I gestured to the vibrant scene around us.

He turned, his surprise evident but his smile disarmingly warm. His voice was smooth and confident. "It's quite something."

Summoning a boldness I typically reserved for business negotiations, I closed the gap between us and reached up, brushing my fingers against the fabric of his coat—high-quality; definitely not from around here—and tugged him towards me. I laced my voice with playful bravado. "Here in Serenity Falls, we're big on making newcomers feel welcome."

His eyes widened, the question in them now unmistakable. But before he could formulate any response, I pulled him down and pressed my lips to his. The kiss wasn't just a peck, either; it was deliberate. A statement.

The man's initial stiffness melted away, his body responding to the unexpected boldness of my gesture. He smelled like crisp, spicy cologne with a subtle undercurrent of citrus, a scent that was as alluring and as out of place in Serenity Falls as a skyscraper.

As I broke the kiss, stepping back with my heart galloping in my chest, I watched his expression shift from surprise to a bemused sort of wonder.

There were no voices in my head this time, no peek into his inner world. Just the lingering taste of cocoa and a hint of mint. Were Tom and Jenna's cases just some bizarre anomaly? Or was I losing touch with reality?

The man stood there, speechless, as if trying to process the unexpected turn of events. His eyes searched mine, probably for some explanation or at least a clue.

I, on the other hand, was already chiding myself. Since when did I kiss strangers at festivals? The last time I did anything remotely this adventurous was... well, trying that new spicy sauce at the Ivy Nook. Hardly the stuff of legends.

He opened his mouth, perhaps to introduce himself or ask who I was, but no words came out. Instead, his broad shoulders slackened, a look of easygoing confusion replacing his initial shock. Despite the bizarre situation, he seemed to exude an air of calm confidence.

"Sorry, no autographs," I said with a smile. Before he could muster a response, I spun on my heels and darted away, leaving him in a daze. My mind was a whirlwind of questions and possibilities.

Was I Serenity Falls's latest mind reader, and this man somehow immune to my newfound ability, or was I just caught in the grip of an overactive imagination?

But for now, duty called. The clock was ticking, and I needed to make my way back to Fireside Manor. My mysterious week-long guest would be arriving soon, and the innkeeper in me knew the importance of a warm welcome.

CHAPTER THREE

THE GUEST

B ack at Fireside Manor, the stage was set for my lone guest's arrival. I'd turned the hospitality dial up to eleven.

I had set him up in my favorite guest room. The Nook was my pièce de résistance. Soft, ambient lighting cast a warm glow over the plush, queen-sized bed, its linens crisp and inviting. On his pillow, I'd placed a small, handcrafted chocolate. Fresh flowers sat in a vase on the bedside table, their fragrance perfuming the air. I'd even gone the extra mile, setting out a personalized welcome note next to a guidebook of Serenity Falls.

As the grandfather clock in the hallway chimed four, my anticipation was tinged with a hint of nervousness. After all, first impressions were key in the B&B business. With a hasty removal of my flour-dusted apron, I took a deep breath to compose myself.

The front door swinging open, bringing with it a gust of frigid air that fluttered the nearby curtains.

I swiveled around, only to be met with the last face I expected—or wanted—to see so soon. Mr. City-Slicker-Kiss himself, suitcase in hand. My mouth opened and closed, mirroring the door chimes. Any semblance of composure I had mustered scrambled out the window, leaving me with a blush that could rival Rudolph's nose.

Well, isn't this a festive plot twist? Here I was, hoping to leave the festival's unique magic behind, and instead, it had followed me home like a lost puppy. A very handsome lost puppy.

A flicker of amusement danced across his eyes. "Seems we're destined to keep running into each other."

I could feel my cheeks warm, a blush that I hoped he'd mistake for the chill in the air. I grabbed his suitcase. "Welcome to Fireside Manor. I promise, ambush kisses are not part of the usual amenities here."

He chuckled, following me into the warmth of the B&B. "I'll hold you to that. Though, I must say, it's not the worst welcome I've ever received." He stuck out his hand. "I'm Ethan."

"Clara." Our hands met, and an electric charge filled the air, tangible as the warmth emanating from the fireplace. His gaze held mine for a moment longer than necessary, sending an unexpected shiver down my spine that definitely had nothing to do with the winter chill.

I masked my reaction with a practiced smile, the innkeeper in me taking the reins. "Right this way." I led him to the registration desk with a professionalism that I hoped would hide the flutter in my stomach. The soft creak of the floorboards under our feet echoed the tentative steps of this new, uncharted interaction.

"I've prepared The Nook for you." I handed him his room key. "It's one of our coziest spaces. And, I promise, no more surprises."

When I handed him his key, something unspoken passed between us—a curiosity, a hint of mutual intrigue. But I tucked away those thoughts, focusing on the here and now. Fireside Manor was my domain, and here, I was all about providing comfort and care, not exploring fleeting connections, no matter how intriguing they might appear. And with a guest? Well, that would just be inappropriate.

Instead of heading straight to his room, Ethan lingered. He seemed unusually captivated by the quirks of the B&B. His eyes roamed over the intricate woodwork of the banister leading upstairs, his hand skimming over the smooth, polished surface. He paused by an antique table, its surface home to an eclectic collection of vintage postcards and a guest book filled with names from around the world. I silently prayed he wouldn't start flipping through to see just how few names. Luckily, he moved on to examine other details of the foyer.

Hmm, either he's a secret aficionado of rustic décor, or that kiss under the mistletoe got to him more than he's letting on. The thought brought a smile to my face. Maybe Mr. City-Slicker wasn't as cool and collected as he appeared. The idea that he might be as flustered as I was felt oddly reassuring.

"Finding everything to your liking?" I watched his reactions closely. The irony of the situation wasn't lost on me. Here I was, the meticulous planner with a cautious heart, escorting the very man I'd impulsively kissed under the guise of an experiment.

No, it *was* an experiment. No guise. None whatsoever. The corners of my mouth twitched involuntarily into a half-smile. Serenity Falls, with its penchant for the unexpected, had outdone itself this time, turning a simple guest check-in into a scene straight out of a novel I would never admit to reading.

"Oh, absolutely." Ethan's voice carried a note of genuine intrigue. "There's a certain... character to this place. It's quite charming."

He then went on to peek into the doorways. Each offered a glimpse into different worlds within the manor: a reading nook bathed in soft light, a sitting room with plush armchairs nestled by a fireplace, and glimpses of ornate tapestries that spoke of a time long past.

I wondered if he was expecting to find a secret passage. Maybe to Narnia. Or to the wine cellar.

His gaze then drifted to the ornate chandelier overhead, its crystals casting playful shadows across the wallpaper, which bore a pattern of delicate roses. Ethan's interest seemed particularly piqued by the old picture frames that adorned the walls, each holding artsy black-and-white photographs of the manor before and during renovation. His fingers brushed against the frames, tracing the contours of history captured within.

"My friend Jenna took those photos," I said. "She wanted to capture the manor's transformation from ghostly grandeur to rustic elegance. She's quite the talent. You might've seen her booth at the festival."

Ethan leaned in, examining a shot of the grand staircase in mid-renovation, draped in dust sheets, its former glory peeking through the chaos. He lingered on it for a moment before turning to me with a thoughtful expression.

"They are remarkable." Ethan's voice carrying a note of genuine admiration. "The way these photographs capture the transition... you can see the soul of the place coming through. Your friend has a real gift for finding beauty in the raw and unrefined."

His compliment made me smile, a warm feeling bubbling up inside. "I'll be sure to pass along your admiration."

Ethan grasped the handle of his suitcase, his smile widened. "Now, about my room—The Nook, was it? Where do I head for some rest and rustic charm?"

"Right this way," I said, leading him up the stairs. "Just wait until you see the room. It's got all the charm of an antique store and none of the mustiness."

Ethan chuckled, the sound warm and easy. "I'll take your word for it. As long as there are no ghostly visitors from a bygone era, I think I'll be quite comfortable."

"Oh, the ghosts only come out on Tuesdays, and they're very polite." I gave him my most charming grin. "They might even offer you some spectral advice on your Christmas shopping list."

We reached his room a bit sooner than I would have liked. "Here you are, your sanctuary from the hustle and bustle of city life. And possibly the occasional friendly ghost."

I stepped back so he could unlock the door. "Just so you know, dinner is at six. And before you ask, no, I don't cook wearing my ghost-whisperer hat."

He smiled, a glint of amusement in his eyes. "I'll be sure not to miss it. Your cooking might just be the highlight of my stay."

I backed away, feeling a mix of relief and curiosity. "Well, settle in. And if you hear any mysterious noises, it's probably just the house settling. Or the ghosts debating the merits of eggnog versus hot cocoa."

Two hours later, the kitchen of Fireside Manor was alive with the rhythmic dance of dinner preparation. I moved with practiced ease, a dash of herbs here, a stir of the pot there, each motion as familiar as the back of my hand. The scent of rosemary and thyme wafted through the air, mingling with the rich aroma of the vegetables cooking on the stove.

The grandfather clock chimed six. That sound was soon followed by the soft tread of footsteps descending the stairs. The moment Ethan appeared in the entryway, the kitchen's atmosphere shifted from tranquil to unmistakably charged. Gone were his sharp city attire and air of urban sophistication. Instead, he wore a simple, well-fitted sweater and a relaxed demeanor. His hair was damp, giving him a more approachable, almost boy-next-door appearance.

I caught myself distracted by the thought of Ethan in the shower, water tracing paths down... *No, Clara, focus. He's a guest, not the lead in your personal Hallmark movie.*

Regaining my composure, I gestured towards the kitchen table. "Make yourself at home. Dinner will be ready in a minute. Can I get you anything? Wine, tea, an EMF detector?" The words tumbled out, laced with a light-heartedness I hoped would mask the brief lapse in my professionalism.

Ethan chuckled, the sound warm and unassuming, as he took a seat at the counter. "Wine sounds great, thanks."

I busied myself with uncorking a bottle of chardonnay. *Okay, Clara, play it cool.* I stole a glance at him. *Just because your guest could double as a Rolex model doesn't mean you get to go all starry-eyed.*

He offered a casual, yet charming smile, clearly more at ease in his less formal guise. "Hope I'm not too underdressed for dinner." His eyes scanned the array of dishes on the counter. "It smells incredible."

I offered a smile, pride swelling in my chest. "Thanks. Homemade meals are of the perks of staying at Fireside Manor. I hope you're hungry." On the counter, a rustic array of comfort food waited to be served. On a cooling tray lay golden, crisp-skinned roast chicken. Beside it, a casserole dish of scalloped potatoes sent up waves of creamy, garlic-infused steam, the top perfectly browned and bubbling. A cast-iron skillet held a medley of sautéed green beans and caramelized shallots, their savory scent mingling with the subtle sweetness of the balsamic glaze.

He nodded, his gaze still lingering on the kitchen's golden hues and the feast in the making. "I haven't had a home-cooked meal in ages."

In the close quarters of the kitchen, we moved together with an unspoken rhythm, filling our plates. The nearness brought a charge of awareness; the brush of his hand against mine while reaching for the serving spoon sent a shiver up my arm.

Guiding Ethan from the kitchen's cozy confines to the dining room, I felt a mix of pride and nervousness. The dining room was all dolled up, its soft lighting making the fine linen and china glow like they were part of a fancy magazine spread.

"Welcome to Fireside Manor's five-star dining experience." I gestured towards the table with a flourish that was maybe a little too dramatic, but hey, why not have a bit of fun with it?

Ethan dropped into his seat, his eyes doing a quick 'holy smokes, this is fancy' scan over my meticulously set table. The candlelight was shamelessly flirting with the silverware and glasses, casting shadows that might as well have been screaming 'romance central!'

And I was internally freaking out. Too over the top? Too romantic? That kiss we had... what if Ethan took it as an all-aboard ticket to love-ville?

I took a deep breath, mentally shooing away those pesky thoughts. *Get a grip, Clara. This is your job, to provide a nice dinner for your guests. It's just two people enjoying a meal. Nothing more.*

As we settled into our chairs, the initial hum of the oven and clatter of pots and pans gave way to the more subdued sounds of clinking glasses and the soft rustle of napkins. I watched Ethan take his first bite, his eyes closing in what I hoped was culinary bliss.

"So, what brings you to our little Serenity Falls?," I asked. "Escaping the city's hustle, or is there more to the story?"

"A bit of both, actually," he said, his voice tinged with a note of nostalgia. "I did need a break from the city's chaos. But I also heard about Serenity Falls's charming traditions, and... well," he hesitated, a distant look in his eyes before he masked it with a polite smile, "I've always been fascinated by small-town histories, the stories that get woven into a place over time."

There was something in the way he said it, a depth that suggested his interest in Serenity Falls wasn't just a casual one. I found myself wanting to ask more, to delve deeper into what stories he hoped to find here, but I held back. It wasn't my place to pry into a guest's personal reasons for visiting, no matter how intriguing they might be.

"I totally get that," I said, my elbows on the table, a forkful of scalloped potatoes paused halfway to my mouth. "In fact, that's part of why I moved here, bought the old manor, and decided to give it a new lease on life. There's just something about Serenity Falls... it's like it has its own heartbeat, you know? A rhythm that's slower, more meaningful."

He nodded, spearing a green bean and glancing around the dining room with an appraising eye. "And I love how you've hung those renovation photos in the lobby. They really do speak to the layers of time and care invested here. It's remarkable, really."

He leaned forward, mirroring my pose. "I'm curious. I love old photos, how they give us peeks into the past. Do you have any of the manor from before its abandonment?" His eyes flicked back to his plate before meeting mine again. "Pictures from when it was in use, perhaps from its early days?"

I put down my fork, my gaze drifting upward as I tried to recall. "You know, I don't think I've come across any," I admitted. "Truth be told, I haven't been able to find much about the manor's past owners or its original purpose. It's like the house sprouted from the ground fully formed as an enigma."

"You don't say?" Ethan's fork clinked softly against his plate as he set it down. "That's quite the mystery. A house with no past. Or at least, one that's hiding it well."

"For all I know, this could have been a speakeasy during Prohibition, a hideout for genteel highwaymen, or even a secret society's meeting place. There's enough hidden nooks and crannies here to fuel a dozen mystery novels. Or, given its secluded location, it could have been a brothel frequented by the upper echelons of society."

He took a sip of wine, eyes reflective. "History has a way of cloaking itself in mystery and grandeur, but the reality is often more...

human, with all its flaws and intricacies. The truth, when uncovered, can often be more complex and, at times, less enchanting."

"True," I agreed, poking at my potatoes. "And come to think of it, it is a bit odd that nobody in town seems to know much about the history of this place."

I wrapped my arms around myself, feeling a sudden chill despite the warmth from the flickering candles. "It's unsettling, really. What if it was something like one of those old homes where families sent away their 'troublesome' relatives? Or, worse, a place where unwed girls were hidden away when they got pregnant, to wait until delivery, knowing their babies would be taken from them. The thought alone is enough to give you the creeps."

"I guess some mysteries are best left unsolved, or else they might just ruin the romantic charm I've worked so hard to create here."

Ethan shifted in his chair, eyes flicking toward the window before returning to his plate. He gave a small, polite smile, but it didn't quite reach his eyes.

My fork froze halfway to my mouth. Oh. Right. I tucked a loose strand of hair behind my ear, suddenly aware of how quiet the room had gotten. The words I'd just spoken echoed back to me, grim and heavy. *Way to set the mood, Clara.*

"Sorry, I didn't mean to get all macabre on you." I cleared my throat and forced a lighter tone into my voice. "You must think this place is run by a lunatic."

Ethan reached for a forkful of scalloped potatoes, his movements unhurried. "Don't worry about it. In fact, a small town mystery is a nice distraction. It's a refreshing change from the chaos of my life back home."

"Oh, but Serenity Falls has its own brand of chaos around the holidays." My fingers fidgeted with the edge of the tablecloth. "The festival is just the beginning."

From across the table, his eyes met mine, holding a flicker of amusement that suggested he remembered our earlier encounter as vividly as I did. The air between us was charged with an unspoken acknowledgment of that moment, adding a layer of complexity to an already intriguing dinner.

"Speaking of the festival," he began, a playful edge to his voice. "About that kiss…"

"Ah, yes, the kiss," I stammered, fumbling with my napkin in a desperate attempt to appear nonchalant. Inside, my mind was racing. *Clara, are you really going to tell him you thought you had turned into some kind of love psychic?*

Gathering my courage, I decided honesty, no matter how bonkers it sounded, was the best policy. Goodness knows I had a distinct lack of that from my past partners. Not that Ethan was a romantic partner. He was just a guest. "That was me conducting a little… experiment."

"Oh?" Ethan leaned forward, his earlier amusement apparently giving way to curiosity.

Taking a deep breath, I plunged into the explanation. "I had this bizarre experience earlier with Tom, the local baker. After a mistletoe-induced peck, I thought I could… hear his thoughts. And then it happened again with my friend Jenna." Saying it aloud, I could hear how absurd it sounded. *Great, Clara, now he's going to think you're completely unhinged.*

His reaction, however, was not what I expected. He didn't laugh or look at me like I had sprouted another head. Instead, he simply nodded, a thoughtful expression on his face. "That's quite a claim. And with me? Did you hear anything?"

A part of me unfurled at his question, and I realized I had been fraying my napkin while I spoke. I just wasn't used to guys taking me seriously. I shook my head. "No, nothing with you. Which only adds to the mystery. It's either a very selective ability or... I'm just imagining things."

Ethan's gaze didn't waver. "Maybe it's the mistletoe itself that's magical." A smile tugged at the corner of his mouth. "After all, you were under it with Tom and Jenna, but not with me."

I raised an eyebrow. "Wow. So you believe in mistletoe magic. Should I be worried you're one of those crystal-carrying moon-water types?"

I meant to be teasing, but I could already hear how my words might land. Too sharp. Too much. My chest tightened, and I glanced away, already waiting for flash of irritation, the clipped tone, the quiet withdrawal that always seemed to follow when I said the wrong thing.

But it didn't come.

Instead, he laughed—a warm, easy sound that softened the edges of my nerves. "Far from it. I'm actually in marketing. Pretty mundane stuff compared to mistletoe magic."

The conversation shifted then, moving away from the realms of magic and mystery and back into the comfortable territory of the here and now. But our 'experiment' lingered between us, a shared secret that somehow brought us closer in the most unexpected of ways.

Perhaps this Ethan guy was different. Not that it mattered. He was a guest, there to enjoy the company and the atmosphere, not to pursue a romantic connection.

CHAPTER FOUR

MISTLETOE MAGIC

The prospect of another evening at the winter festival hadn't initially been on my agenda. So why was I contemplating the invitation Ethan had laid before me with nonchalant charm?

"Come on, Clara, the tree-lighting ceremony is something you can't miss," he'd said, with an enthusiasm that was both adorable and infectious.

I pretended to mull it over, putting on a show of reluctance. "Well, I suppose I could make an exception." I finally conceded, though a part of me was looking forward to it. Spending time with Ethan was proving to be an unexpected highlight in my otherwise predictable routine.

The day had unfolded in a series of simple yet pleasant moments. We'd started with a leisurely breakfast in Fireside Manor's sunlit breakfast room, where Ethan had shown an almost comical fascination with everything from the secret behind my blueberry jam to the architectural structure of the B&B. And when he popped the question—no, not that one—asking if I'd play tour guide, I thought, *why not?* After all, he was my sole guest, and rolling out the red carpet seemed like good business. A glowing review would be just the cherry on top. Let's be clear, my agreement had absolutely nothing to do with his dashing looks or the way my heart did a little salsa dance whenever he smiled.

Later, a stroll through Serenity Falls's streets, lined with shops and the occasional waft of pine, had led us to a café. Over cups of steaming hot chocolate, Ethan had shared snippets of his life in the city, while I offered tales of small-town quirks and characters. With each shared story and burst of laughter, a sense of connection grew between us, a companionship that was as unexpected as it was enjoyable.

Now, as we prepared to join the festivities of the evening, I realized that a comfortable ease had settled between us. It was a feeling I hadn't known I'd missed, and part of me wondered what the rest of the evening would hold.

Before heading downstairs, I paused in front of the mirror, taking a moment to assess my reflection. The woman staring back at me had always been more comfortable wrapped in the cocoon of her B&B, but tonight she looked... different.

My eyes, a deep shade of hazel, held a hint of anticipation, framed by the soft blonde waves that fell just past my shoulders. Tucking a rebellious strand behind my ear, I noticed how nicely it contrasted with my freckled skin.

"Just keep it professional, Clara," I reminded myself sternly, even as a small smile played on my lips. "He's a guest, not a holiday romance."

Memories unbidden crept into my mind, echoes of past relationships that had started with sparks like these only to burn out, leaving a trail of disappointment and a heart more guarded each time. There was Alex, whose laughter filled my days until his wanderlust pulled him away. Brian, the charming artist who tried to steal from me to fund his tuition. And then there was Julian, the one I had thought was the one, until one day, he simply wasn't. His betrayal had not just broken my heart but had shattered my trust, pushing me to seek refuge in a place where the past couldn't reach me.

I had emerged from all of it wiser, more independent, but undeniably more cautious. The idea of a Christmas fling, light and without expectations, seemed almost tempting in its simplicity. But experience had taught me that even the lightest of flings could leave a lasting imprint, and I wasn't sure I was ready for another.

So, as I applied the final touches to my makeup, I fortified my resolve with a dash of skepticism. Tonight was about the joy of the season, not about igniting a flame that could all too easily turn into a fire I wasn't prepared to handle.

A practical thought struck me then, a businesswoman's silver lining to the evening's outing. The festival would still be brimming with potential guests, people who might just be charmed enough by Serenity Falls's festive spirit to seek out a cozy place to stay. People who may not have gotten a cookie last night. I could use tonight as another marketing opportunity for Fireside Manor.

With a renewed sense of purpose, I reached for a stack of business cards from the dresser. Slipping a handful into my purse, I felt a bit more in control, a bit more like the savvy entrepreneur I was. Tonight, I would be the gracious hostess of Fireside Manor, spreading cheer and, perhaps, drumming up some business in the process.

I took one last look in the mirror. My outfit for the evening was simple yet elegant: a forest green sweater-dress that hugged my curves, paired with comfortable ankle boots—practical for walking, yet stylish enough for the festival. A delicate silver necklace lay against my collarbone, its pendant catching the light as I moved. Sexy, yet professional.

Ready now, with both my makeup and my marketing materials in place, I took a deep breath and left the bathroom. Descending the stairs, I could feel the softness of the dress against my skin.

As I reached the bottom, I caught Ethan's gaze. His expression was a blend of admiration and a touch of surprise, as if the transformation from everyday innkeeper to the figure standing before him was more than he'd bargained for. *Yes, Ethan, the woman who fluffs your pillows also happens to clean up quite nicely.*

He stood up, a reflex of politeness or perhaps something more, his eyes following me as I approached. "Clara," he said, his voice a touch softer, a shade more intimate than before. "You look... incredible."

There was a certain satisfaction in seeing that look on his face. For a heartbeat, I allowed myself to bask in the warmth of his compliment.

"Thank you, Ethan," I replied, the hostess in me taking the reins once more. "Shall we head out? The festival won't experience itself."

The winter festival was in full swing when we arrived, the air buzzing with excitement and the sweet scent of hot cider. The square was a riot of lights, laughter, and melodies. The grand tree stood tall, awaiting its moment of glory when they flipped on the lights.

As soon as we entered the fray, Tom spotted us from across the square, his approach unavoidable. A knot of worry tightened in my stomach. Hopefully he didn't get the wrong idea about that mistletoe kiss last night.

"Clara, you heartbreaker!" Tom called out, his eyes twinkling with mischief as he approached. "I was all set to snag another mistletoe kiss, and you've moved on to this charming stranger."

I felt my cheeks warm, but I donned my best innkeeper's smile. "Ethan here is simply enjoying the renowned hospitality of Fireside Manor."

Tom chuckled. "Sure he is. Enjoy the festival, you two." He tipped an imaginary hat before wandering off to undoubtedly share this new tidbit with the rest of Serenity Falls.

As we mingled through the crowd, I couldn't shake off the uneasy feeling Tom's words had stirred. Was I being reckless, blurring the lines between professional and personal? Yet, as I glanced at Ethan, who was marveling at the charm of our little town, I felt a sense of rightness that was hard to ignore.

We soon found ourselves in line for cider, the quintessential festival treat. Ethan was sharing a story about his first encounter with winter in the city. While laughing at his tale, my eyes casually swept over the crowd, only to pause on a particularly striking sight: Doris, hat festooned with twinkling Christmas lights.

Upon spotting us, her eyes sparkled as brightly as her hat. She gave a knowing nod and a sly, almost conspiratorial wink in our direction. Had she witnessed our kiss the night before? It hadn't exactly been a private affair, but part of me had clung to the hope it had gone unnoticed.

I might as well have announced my moment with Ethan on the town bulletin board.

I stifled a sigh. "Looks like we've got company," I murmured to Ethan, nodding subtly towards Doris. Her presence was a reminder of the small-town microscope under which every interaction was scrutinized and misinterpreted.

Ethan followed my gaze, a hint of amusement in his eyes as he caught sight of Doris. "The plot thickens," he said. "Is this where I should expect the town newsletter to feature a special on the mysterious out-of-towner and the innkeeper?"

I laughed, the tension easing. "You might just become Serenity Falls's next headline."

With warm cups of cider in hand, we wove our way towards the center of the festival, where the tree lighting was set to take place. As we passed Doris, I offered her a polite smile, which she returned with a knowing look. There was a certain art to navigating small-town social nuances, a way of offering subtle acknowledgment without inviting too much scrutiny.

Our stroll through the festival took an unexpected turn when we found ourselves under the old oak tree, face to face with the town curmudgeon, Harold Jenkins. His weathered face, marked by deep lines of time and a habitual frown, was even more pronounced under the tree's gnarled branches. The stark white of his hair, unkempt and thinning, contrasted sharply with his dark, heavy overcoat, making him appear as a relic from a bygone era amidst the festival's vibrancy.

"Evening, Mr. Jenkins," I greeted, my voice wary as I took in his piercing eyes, which seemed to miss nothing despite their age-softened hue. His hands, gnarled like the branches above us, were clasped in front of him, a physical barrier to the world's cheer.

"Clara," he responded gruffly before shifting his gaze to Ethan. The skepticism in his eyes was as clear as the frosty air. "Another guest charmed by Fireside Manor, I see."

Ethan, seemingly unfazed by Mr. Jenkins' brusque demeanor, stepped forward with a confidence that was both respectful and disarming.

"Ethan Morris," he said, extending a hand that Jenkins regarded for a moment before accepting with a reluctant, rough grip. "Indeed, the charm of Fireside Manor is hard to resist."

"Harold Jenkins." A grunt escaped Mr. Jenkins, a sound that, in its brevity, seemed to convey a begrudging acknowledgment. His gaze lingered on us for a moment longer, the ghost of countless winters reflected in his eyes, before he nodded curtly and turned his attention back to the oak tree, as solitary and enduring as himself.

I excused myself and headed back toward the festival. Ethan tugged me close, his eyes alighting on something above Mr. Jenkins.

I followed his gaze and saw the mistletoe hanging there, its presence both ominous and intriguing. He leaned in, a mischievous glint in his eye. "Clara, what if you tried the mistletoe experiment with Harold? Just to test our theory."

The suggestion took me aback. The thought of kissing Harold Jenkins, even for 'scientific' purposes, was both ludicrous and strangely compelling. After a moment's hesitation, driven by a blend of curiosity and Ethan's encouraging smile, I approached the man once more.

"Mr. Jenkins, would you mind partaking in a little Serenity Falls tradition with me?" I pointed to the mistletoe above us.

To my surprise, Mr. Jenkins, after a brief, stunned pause, cracked a small, almost wistful smile. "Well, I suppose one must uphold tradition."

As my lips brushed his cheek, it was like opening a long-sealed door to the past. A deluge of thoughts and emotions cascaded into my mind. I saw a young girl, maybe sixteen, bathed in moonlight, her laugh echoing like a melody in the still night. Stolen moments of tender affection, hidden away from prying eyes, filled with whispers and gentle caresses. The profound longing in his heart, the ache of unsaid words, swirled around me. And then, the letter, worn and faded in his memories, never sent, words of a love unconfessed and a future unexplored.

These fragments painted a picture of a love story, a poignant tale of deep affection and silent yearning that Harold had kept buried deep within his heart for years. It was a love of quiet intensity, marked by moments of shared secrets and unspoken promises, a connection that time had not dimmed but life had forced to remain hidden.

As I pulled away, the intensity of Harold Jenkins' long-hidden emotions left me breathless. My eyes sought Ethan's, wide with the shock and revelation of what had just happened. In that brief kiss,

I had witnessed the tender side of a man who had spent a lifetime concealing his deepest feelings, guarding a love story that could have been, but never was.

After a moment of shared silence, Harold cleared his throat, the familiar gruffness returning to his voice. "Well, I should be getting on. Thank you for the... hospitality." He hesitated, then, in an uncharacteristic gesture, extended his arms for a brief, awkward hug.

"Of course. Take care." I returned the embrace with a gentle pat on his back. As he turned and walked away, a part of me felt connected to the hidden chapters of his life, stories untold yet deeply felt.

After our unexpected encounter under the mistletoe with Harold Jenkins, Ethan and I drifted away from the oak tree, leaving its canopy of memories behind. I was in such a state of shock as we maneuvered our way through the crowd, I barely noticed the scent of pine and the sound of music that surrounded us. The chatter and laughter of the townsfolk created a lively backdrop to our own shared experience. Everyone's steps gradually converged towards the center of the square.

The grand Christmas tree, adorned with countless lights, stood as the centerpiece. The festive atmosphere was infectious, and despite the swirl of emotions and revelations, I found myself caught up in the excitement. It was as if the entire town of Serenity Falls had gathered to not just witness the lighting of the tree, but to be part of a moment that symbolized the heart and soul of our community during the holiday season.

Beside me, Ethan leaned in, his eyes reflecting the shimmering spectacle. Our eyes met, and in that brief exchange, a world of unspoken conversation passed between us. It was as though the crowd, with their anticipatory chatter, faded into a distant murmur, leaving just the two of us in our own secluded bubble. The mayor took the microphone and began a speech, but I paid it no attention.

"Ethan," I whispered, finally finding my voice. I leaned in. "When I kissed Mr. Jenkins under the mistletoe... I saw something, his thoughts or memories."

"What did you see?"

"It was like echoes from the past," I said, my voice barely above a whisper amidst the festive commotion. "Fragments of a high school romance, lost love letters, secret moments. It felt so real."

I paused, the weight of the revelation still settling in. "You were right. The mistletoe is the key. But its magic, or whatever this is, it's getting stronger. With each kiss, it's like I'm diving deeper into someone else's heart, uncovering secrets that were never meant to be seen."

Ethan's gaze deepened. "That's incredible, Clara. What are you going to do now?"

The lights flickered to life, and a hush momentarily fell over the town square. It was as if time itself had paused, every breath and heartbeat synchronized with the illuminating bulbs. The glow bathed the square in a warm, enchanting light, transforming the ordinary into the extraordinary.

As the surrounding crowd erupted into applause, the bubble of our conversation burst, bringing me back to the reality of the here and now. I was an innkeeper, grounded and pragmatic. And Ethan, with his now apparent connection to my bizarre mistletoe mystery, was a guest, an intriguing part of my world that was both exciting and unnerving.

But as I stood there, under the canopy of lights, I couldn't deny the thrill of discovery, the stirring of something that went beyond the boundaries I had so carefully constructed around my life. This unexpected journey into the past was turning into more than just a fleeting chapter in my story. It was becoming a tale of its own, intertwined with a mystery that wove through the very heart of Serenity Falls.

A story of love lost to time.

CHAPTER FIVE

THE COZY CUP

The Cozy Cup was a hive of activity, with every table occupied by early risers seeking their caffeine fix. The windows were charmingly fogged, blurring the snowy world outside. Ethan and I found a small table in a quiet corner, the aroma of coffee and Tom's elderberry pastries wrapping around us like a comforting blanket.

I lifted my pastry, admiring its perfect, flaky layers, and took a bite. "This was a great idea. Thank you for suggesting it."

After our late night at the festival, Ethan had been adamant about giving me a respite from my B&B breakfast routine.

"You deserve a morning off, Clara," he said with that easy smile of his.

"I deserve every morning off." I took a bite of my pastry. "So, you're taking over breakfast duties for the rest of your stay, right?"

Ethan put on a grave face and leaned in. "Absolutely. Prepare to be amazed. Back home, my culinary expertise extends to an avant-garde dish I like to call The Toasted Bread Experience. It's bread, but get this...toasted."

My laughter filled the air. "Are you vying for a job as chef at the manor? How will I ever match that level of gourmet cooking?"

"It's all in the wrist action. The perfect flip, the precise timing. It's an art form."

I grinned, taking another bite of my pastry. "Well, Ethan, I look forward to being dazzled by your toast-flipping skills."

"Indeed." Ethan's voice was laden with mock seriousness. "I mean, after seeing Tom's expression last night when he caught us together, I did start to wonder... Maybe his pastries are his way of vying for your affections? You know, a romantic showdown. Me, with my charming wit and debonair demeanor—"

"And don't forget the toast—"

"...and Tom, with his... dough."

I burst into laughter at his theatrical portrayal of a rivalry, then set to work polishing off the rich, sweet elderberry swirl. The playful banter with Ethan had lightened the mood, but as I stirred my coffee, my thoughts drifted back to the more serious matters at hand. The clink of the spoon against the mug seemed to echo the weight of Jenna's unspoken love for Maggie and the haunting, unresolved story of Harold Jenkins' past.

There was a sense of purpose brewing inside me, a desire to unravel these hidden stories. Maybe this mistletoe magic, this unexpected ability to glimpse into others' hearts, had come to me for a reason. Perhaps I was meant to uncover these hidden stories, to bring closure to people who had long since given up.

Maggie now lived on the other side of the country, which was not ideal. Long-distance romances were even more tenuous than everyday ones. It was too bad, really. But Mr. Jenkins was a puzzle I could—

"You seem deep in thought, Clara." The corners of Ethan's mouth twitched. "You're not considering running off with Tom after this impressive display of pastry skills, are you? I haven't even had the chance to showcase my toast-making prowess."

"Actually, yes. Tom and I are planning a baking-themed wedding. We'll have a cinnamon roll tiered cake, croissant bouquets, and a vow exchange over a flour-dusted altar. It's going to be the sweetest ceremony ever—quite literally."

Ethan nodded sagely. "Ah, I see. This is a shotgun wedding situation, isn't it? You've got a cinnamon bun of your own in the oven. Tom moves quickly. Or does this mistletoe magic do more than just show you lost loves?"

I chuckled at Ethan's playful remark, but then sighed , the lightness in my heart fading as the weight of reality settled back in. I absentmindedly traced the rim of my coffee cup with my finger. "The mistletoe... it's been revealing more than I expected. Mr. Jenkins' story is haunting me. Unresolved love has a peculiar way of clinging to your thoughts, doesn't it? It's like they're pleading for something. Closure, maybe. Or understanding."

Ethan leaned forward, his eyes, a deep blend of curiosity and earnestness, locked onto mine. "Or maybe you're supposed to reunite these lost loves."

I felt a flutter of something inexplicable as I met his gaze, a skeptical smile tugging at my lips. "Reunite them? That seems a bit... futile, don't you think? Relationships end for a reason." To my surprise, my words were laced with a hint of challenge, almost inviting him to contradict me.

"Maybe it's a lesson for you," said Ethan. "To see that love can be more resilient, more enduring than you've given it credit."

The intensity of his gaze held mine, and for a moment, the world outside the window, with its snowflakes kissing the ground, made me believe him. But I shook that off and let out a disbelieving laugh. "Maybe fate's playing a joke on me—casting me, the least likely believer in happily-ever-afters, as the town's heart-healer. What's next? Cupid asking for archery tips?"

Ethan's laughter, rich and warm, melded with mine, filling the space around us with a comfort that felt dangerously close to intimacy. "A matchmaker who doesn't believe in matches," he mused. "It's like a vegetarian being a barbecue judge."

I rolled my eyes, a playful gesture to mask the quickening of my pulse. Picking up my coffee, I took a sip, fully aware of Ethan's gaze still fixed on me. "Exactly. I'm the culinary critic who can't stand the kitchen heat. And yet, here I am, apron tied and all, on the verge of getting burned."

Are we still talking about Mr. Jenkins, or has this conversation subtly sautéed into something a bit more... personal?

Ethan's gaze softened, the corners of his mouth still curved in a lingering smile. "Or, perhaps, you'll find a new recipe for love, one that even a skeptic like you can believe in."

His words, tender and hopeful, reverberated in my mind. They definitely felt less like a comment on my mistletoe escapades and more like a gentle nudge into a territory I hadn't charted on my maps yet. How had we segued from the town's heartaches to what felt suspiciously like the beginnings of a rom-com plotline? Was this the universe's way of tossing me into the deep end of the love pool to see if I'd swim?

As I pondered this, I noticed Ethan's shift in posture. He leaned forward, his demeanor changing from playful to business-like. "So, Clara, how do you propose we approach this investigation? What's our first step?"

I blinked, taken aback by his assumption. Ethan's straightforward plunge into planning caught me off guard. Not only had he seamlessly transitioned into discussing our next steps, but he also seemed to have firmly placed himself as my partner in this unexpected venture.

"Ethan, wait a minute," I said, my eyebrows arching in surprise. "You're serious about this? I mean, I thought you were here to enjoy your holiday, not to get tangled up in finding the lost love of the town curmudgeon."

His response came with a lighthearted yet sincere smile. "I can't think of a better way to spend my vacation than helping you uncover these mysteries. And besides, diving into Harold's story sounds far more intriguing than the usual tourist activities."

I studied him for a moment, still trying to wrap my head around his eagerness to jump into this with me. It was one thing to chat over coffee about the peculiar twists of fate and the heart, but quite another to embark on a mission to untangle the delicate threads of someone's past love. Yet, Ethan seemed ready and willing to dive into the deep end with me.

"Alright," I conceded, a smile tugging at the corners of my mouth. "If you're in, then I'm in."

As Ethan nodded in agreement, I found myself both surprised and quietly thrilled at the prospect of having him by my side in this unexpected journey. Maybe, just maybe, this holiday season was about to become a lot more interesting.

The rhythmic clink of spoons against coffee cups filled the air as we sat in the corner of the diner. I sipped my coffee, relishing its rich warmth, as Ethan seemed to ponder our next move.

"So," said Ethan as he stirred his coffee, "do we go straight to the source? Should we just ask Mr. Jenkins about these letters?" His eyes met mine across the steam rising from our cups, holding a glint of shared curiosity and something else, something I wasn't quite ready to name.

I took a sip of my coffee, feeling the warmth spread through me, not just from the drink but from Ethan's gaze. "Direct might be best, but Harold Jenkins is about as approachable as a hedgehog. And given that this involves matters of the heart..." I hesitated, my skepticism about love clashing with the unexpected flutter in my stomach.

Ethan's gaze lingered on me, a smile playing on his lips as he contemplated my words. "I suppose asking around town might draw unwanted attention. Especially if we mention it to the wrong person."

"Like Doris," I added with a wry smile. "Though she's a well-spring of town history, telling her would be like hosting a town meeting. She's the absolute last person we'd want to go to with this investigation." I surreptitiously swept the room for any sign of the woman, struck with a sudden fear that reciting Doris's name out loud might summon her. Fortunately, the coast was clear of her prying presence. At least that's one less thing to worry about.

Ethan's laugh was warm, the sound sending an unexpected thrill through me. "Right. Maybe there's someone else in his life? Friends or family?"

I shook my head, a strand of hair falling across my face. Ethan's hand twitched, as if he wanted to reach out and tuck it behind my ear, but he refrained. "Harold's always been a bit of a lone wolf. No family that anyone knows of, and friends are... well, let's just say, he's not the social butterfly type."

Just then, the café door burst open, letting in a brisk gust of winter air that danced through the Cozy Cup, playfully disturbing its warm embrace. Into this cheerful chaos stepped Ms. Hattie. Her stature, though modest, was complemented by an air of grace and resilience—the kind that turned heads without trying.

She paused at the threshold, brushing snowflakes from her deep plum coat, the flakes clinging like white petals against the rich wool. The scent of cocoa butter and cold air followed her in, familiar and comforting. A knitted hat, clearly handmade, hugged her head, and from beneath it peeked elegant coils of silver hair, glinting in the light like spun frost.

As she closed the door behind her with a gentle nudge, silvery strands of hair peeked out from beneath her lovingly knitted hat.

A few patrons lit up at the sight of her, offering nods and warm greetings. Ms. Hattie returned them with a smile that crinkled the corners of her eyes—eyes that had seen plenty, and still sparkled. She stepped into the line with the calm assurance of someone who'd long since learned the art of moving through the world with dignity. Each step was deliberate, her posture regal despite the weight of the years she carried.

"Ethan," I whispered, leaning across the table. "Ms. Hattie is about Harold's age. And she's been in this town forever, from what I've heard. It's possible she and Harold grew up together, right?"

Ethan followed my gaze, his expression turning thoughtful. "That's a great point. If anyone knows the stories of the past, it could be her."

My mind raced with the possibilities. Ms. Hattie might hold the key to understanding Mr. Jenkins' enigmatic past. She could be our link to the untold stories that the mistletoe had hinted at. A bridge to the bygone days of Serenity Falls.

As she placed her order and found a table near the window, I exchanged a look with Ethan. "Should we talk to her? Casually, of course. Maybe she can shed some light on Harold without even realizing it."

Ethan nodded, a spark of excitement in his eyes. "Let's do it. But let's be subtle. We don't want to spook her or make her feel like she's being interrogated. Ease into the conversation. I mean, for all we know, Ms. Hattie *is* Harold's long-lost love."

I shook my head. "Pretty sure she's not. The woman in his memories was white."

"Fair enough. Still, let's keep it casual. Just a little curiosity, nothing too obvious."

I took a deep breath, bolstered by Ethan's presence and our shared mission. "Subtle. Right. I can do subtle."

Without waiting for a strategic plan to form, I stood, my chair scraping against the floor a little too loudly. I marched over to Ms. Hattie's table, my strides determined.

She looked up, her expression one of mild surprise as I approached.

"Ms. Hattie, hi! Mind if we join you for a bit?" I asked, my voice several notches higher than intended.

Ethan, trailing behind me, offered a polite smile that clearly said, 'I'm sorry for whatever is about to happen here.'

She peered up at me, her eyes twinkling with curiosity. "Well, sure, dear. I don't see why not."

"So," I began, leaning in as if about to share a state secret. "You've been in Serenity Falls a long time, haven't you? I bet you've seen all sorts of things, know all sorts of stories... and secrets, like maybe sordid affairs or tales of lost loves?"

Ethan coughed.

"Well, dear, I have been around for a while. Seen a lot, heard a lot. Serenity Falls is a small place, but it's got its share of tales." A smile crept onto Ms. Hattie's lips. "Clara, are you branching out from the B&B to become a historian?"

I laughed, a bit too nervously, trying to steer the conversation with some semblance of subtlety. "Oh, no, just curious about the town's history. Harold Jenkins, for example. He seems like he'd have a story or two."

Ethan quietly facepalmed behind his coffee cup while Ms. Hattie regarded me with a look that was equal parts amused and intrigued. "Harold Jenkins, you say? Now that's a name I haven't heard in a conversation for a while. What's the sudden interest in old Harold?"

I glanced at Ethan, whose expression was a mix of 'abort mission' and reluctant curiosity, then turned back to Ms. Hattie. But historian? That gave me an idea. "Oh, just a little project of ours. We're, uh, mapping the romantic history of Serenity Falls. For... posterity."

Ms. Hattie's laugh was rich and knowing. "Well, isn't that something? I might have a tale or two, but you'll have to promise to keep it between us. Town secrets, you know."

As she began to speak, I realized that our 'subtle' approach might have been the perfect misstep, leading us right where we needed to be.

I leaned towards Ms. Hattie, my curiosity piqued. "Did you go to school with Harold? What was he like back then?"

Ms. Hattie nodded, a hint of nostalgia in her eyes. "Oh, yes, Harold and I were in the same class. He was always a bit of a loner, you know. Quiet, kept to himself. We weren't close, but you could always find him with his nose in a book or wandering the school grounds alone."

Ethan, picking up on the thread, leaned in. "Did he ever have a sweetheart? Anyone he was close to?"

Ms. Hattie's expression turned thoughtful. "No, not that I ever knew of. Harold had his family obligations. His mother was ill for a long time, and he devoted much of his time to taking care of her. That sort of thing didn't leave much room for teenage romance, I suppose."

Her words painted a picture of Harold's youth marked by responsibility and solitude. It was a revelation that added depth to the enigmatic figure of Mr. Jenkins and perhaps a clue to the puzzle of his lost love.

"That explains a lot," I mused aloud, my mind turning over this new information. "Taking care of a sick parent must have been hard. It sounds like he had to grow up too fast, missing out on those carefree days of youth. Maybe that's why he's so reserved now."

"That makes sense." Ethan's tone carried a hint of something deeper, a note of personal understanding that piqued my curiosity. His expression, usually so open and amiable, briefly flickered with a shadow. For a moment, I wondered about the paths Ethan had walked, the turns his life had taken. Would a mistletoe kiss reveal the secrets he carries? The thought was tempting, for more reasons than one.

As Ms. Hattie took a sip of her coffee, a distant look of remembrance crossed her face. "You know, if you're really interested in Harold Jenkins, you might consider speaking with Edna Simmons. Now that I think about it, back in their high school days, she was about the only person Harold ever spent any real time with. At least for a while. Not sure what happened there."

Intrigued, I leaned forward, the mention of Edna Simmons sparking a connection in my mind. "Edna Simmons... I've heard of her. Wasn't she the one who used to organize all those charity balls back in the day?" I asked, trying to piece together the fragments of Serenity Falls's history I'd picked up over the last two years.

Ms. Hattie nodded. "Edna Simmons was a real pillar of the community. These days, you'll find her at the community center, usually deep in her bridge games. She's got a memory like a vault, especially for the old days."

I smiled warmly at Ms. Hattie. "Thank you so much for your time and insights, Ms. Hattie. You've been incredibly helpful."

Ethan echoed my thanks with a polite nod, his expression thoughtful.

Ms. Hattie waved off our thanks with a chuckle. "Always happy to share a bit of history with the younger generation. Good luck with your little investigation," she said with a wink.

We stood, leaving the café's warm ambiance and smell of coffee and pastries. Stepping outside, the cold air greeted us like a brisk reminder of the world moving beyond the comfortable confines of the Cozy Cup.

On the sidewalk, Ethan and I paused and exchanged a look. A new avenue of inquiry had opened up before us. "Edna Simmons," I said, my breath forming a misty cloud in the chilly air. "Could she be the mystery woman in Harold's past?"

CHAPTER SIX

COMMUNITY CENTER

The Serenity Falls Community Center was bursting with festive cheer, its walls echoing with a blend of lively activity and Christmas melodies. As Ethan and I stepped inside, the grandeur of a beautifully decorated Christmas tree in the foyer captivated my attention. Adorned with twinkling lights, handmade ornaments, and strands of silver tinsel, it stood as a monument to the season's joy.

"Looks like they've pulled out all the stops for Christmas," I remarked, admiring the tree's shimmering lights.

Ethan's eyes followed the garlands that adorned the walls. "It's like stepping into a holiday postcard. You've got to admit, there's something about Christmas that just brings out the romance in everything."

I shot him a playful glance. "Romance? At Christmas? It's more a season of frantic shopping and endless to-do lists if you ask me."

He raised an eyebrow, a smile playing on his lips. "Cynical much, Clara? Come on, even you have to admit there's a certain magic in the air. Just look around."

We moved deeper into the community center, where the festive spirit had clearly taken root. Elderly couples and clusters of friends gathered around tables, laughing over card games and swapping stories, while the soft strains of a Christmas classic drifted from hidden speakers. The whole place felt alive with nostalgia, laughter, and just enough sparkle to make even a skeptic smile.

"Okay, maybe there's a bit of magic," I conceded. "But I'll reserve judgment on the romance part."

Ethan's laugh was light and infectious, and for a moment, I allowed myself to be swept up in the festive spirit that filled the community center.

Near one of the large windows, framed by curtains that cascaded in rich hues of red and gold, sat an elderly couple that seemed to embody a timeless romance. The man, with his hair turned the shade of winter snow, gazed at his companion with eyes still bright with affection. Beside him, the woman, her silver hair styled fashionably, laughed at something he said, the creases around her eyes telling tales of countless smiles shared over the years.

Their hands were entwined on the table, fingers interlocked with the ease of decades spent together. Between them sat a poinsettia, its vibrant red petals adding a dash of color to their quiet corner. The way they leaned towards each other, the unspoken understanding in their glances, and the tender way he brushed a stray lock of hair from her face—all these little gestures wove a story of deep, enduring love.

A warmth, unfamiliar and unsettling, flickered in my chest, painting images of a future filled with such quiet tenderness. It was a scene from a story I had long told myself was not meant for me. But as their laughter, soft and harmonious, drifted across the room, a shadow fell across these fleeting thoughts. The old fear, like a quiet specter, whispered reminders of past hurts, of the risk of giving one's heart only to have it returned in pieces.

A quick glance at Ethan, who was now studying a poster on the wall, anchored me back to reality. The ease in his stance, the gentle curve of his smile. They were here and now—tangible, real, and without the daunting promise of forever. The thought of exploring anything deeper with him danced at the edge of my mind, a step too far from the safety of the shore I clung to.

Resolutely, I shifted my focus back to the mystery of Harold's past love. That's why we were here, after all. The comfort of the unsolved and the known was a balm to the quiet stirrings of hope I was not yet ready to face.

Shaking off the lingering thoughts of what could be, I nudged Ethan. "Let's find Edna."

Ethan glanced around the bustling room, then turned back to me. "What does she look like?"

I thought for a moment. "Well, Edna's in her late seventies, I'd say. She's got that kind of timeless look—silver hair, always neatly done... usually wears comfortable clothes, nothing too flashy."

Ethan scanned the community center, his gaze flitting from one person to the next. A smirk played on his lips as he turned back to me. "Clara, that description could match nearly every woman here."

"You're right." I laughed, racking my brain for a more distinctive portrayal of Edna. "Well, my talent clearly doesn't lie in playing the part of a sketch artist. Describing people is more challenging than baking a perfect soufflé. And that's saying something."

As we scanned the bustling room, our attention was drawn to a table where a lively game of bridge was underway. Amidst the group, one woman stood out with her infectious laughter and spirited gestures. She animatedly chided her partner, her vibrant energy infusing the air around her. Dressed elegantly in a classic pearl gray sweater, she exuded a poise and grace that spoke of a bygone era of sophistication. Her hair, a soft shade of silver, was styled in a graceful wave, perfectly framing a face that sparkled with intelligence. Her twinkling eyes reflected a keen wit.

Just as we were observing her, one of her bridge partners leaned in, a smile on her face, and said, "Oh, Edna, you always know how to make these games interesting!"

For a moment, I paused, my gaze shifting between the vivacious woman at the table and the solitary and reserved person that is Harold Jenkins. The contrast was striking, almost jarring, like pairing a vibrant painting with a somber photograph.

"That's Edna Simmons?" Ethan whispered, his eyes reflecting the buzz of our shared discovery.

I nodded, a smile tugging at my lips. I took a steadying breath and stepped forward, trying to calm the flutter of nerves in my chest. This felt important, like something I needed to see through. Ever since the mistletoe moment, things had started lining up in a way I couldn't ignore. Meeting Edna Simmons, digging into Harold Jenkins' past... it felt like something I was meant to do. Like maybe these stories were waiting for someone to listen. And somehow, that someone had become me.

I took a steadying breath and approached Edna. "Excuse me, Edna?"

She turned, a look of mild surprise crossing her face. "Yes, dear?"

I offered a warm smile, trying to ease into the conversation naturally. "I'm Clara Winters from Fireside Manor. I was wondering if you might have a minute? There's something I'd love to chat with you about, if you don't mind."

Edna's expression shifted to one of curiosity as she nodded, "Of course, dear. I was just about to head back to my apartment. Care to join me for some tea?"

Edna unlocked the door to her apartment nestled within the retirement village. As soon as we stepped inside, Edna, embodying the grace of a hostess from a more genteel time, set about preparing tea. The apartment was a cozy haven, with delicate lace curtains filtering the afternoon light.

The air soon became perfumed with the comforting scent of Earl Grey, mingling with a hint of lavender emanating from a nearby potpourri dish. Ethan and I exchanged glances, silently acknowledging the charm of the place.

The room was a patchwork of times gone by, with walls adorned in photographs that spoke of decades rich with experience. Plush armchairs, draped in crocheted blankets and pillows, beckoned invitingly. Shelves lined with well-thumbed books and trinkets hinted at a life lived with curiosity and affection for the past. It was a small haven brimming with memories.

I took a seat, my eyes idly tracing the patterns of the crochet work, pondering the stories each loop might hold. "So," I began, as Edna handed us our teacups with a flourish fit for royalty. "We hear you were quite the social butterfly back in high school. Did Harold Jenkins ever flutter into your circle?"

Edna took a sip of her tea, eyeing us over the rim of her cup with an inquisitive gaze. "Now, what brings Harold Jenkins to mind for you two? It's not every day that folks come asking about him."

Ethan exchanged a quick, conspiratorial glance with me before responding. "We saw him at the festival, standing alone under the mistletoe. It piqued our curiosity, you know, seeing such a reserved figure amidst all that celebration."

I chimed in, adding a layer of casual interest to our inquiry. "Yes, it got us wondering about the man behind the solitary facade. Harold always seems so... enigmatic. We thought perhaps there was more to his story, especially his younger days."

Edna leaned back, her eyes narrowing. "Ah, the mistletoe. That does have a way of stirring up old memories and what-ifs, doesn't it?" She paused, her gaze becoming distant, as if she were sifting through the sands of time. "Harold was indeed a different person back then. More than most people in Serenity Falls realize."

The anticipation in the room thickened, like the plot of a novel at the brink of a pivotal revelation.

Edna set her teacup down with a gentle clink, her eyes reflecting the flicker of memories. "Harold and I shared quite a few classes. He was always the quiet one, more comfortable in the library than at a dance. But he had a depth to him that few took the time to notice."

I leaned forward, my curiosity piqued. "And how did you get to know Harold?"

Her smile deepened. "It was during our sophomore year. Our literature class had been assigned a group project, and by some stroke of fate, Harold and I ended up as partners. That's when I met Harold few knew. He had this rich understanding of literature, an ability to see beyond the words on the page."

Ethan and I exchanged a glance. Edna's voice held a warmth and fondness that spoke of more than just a classmate's casual remembrance.

As I listened, a realization dawned on me, as clear and startling as the first winter frost. The way we had been led to Edna, so swiftly and naturally, it couldn't be mere coincidence. The mystery of Harold Jenkins was unfolding before us with an ease that felt almost preordained, as if the mistletoe knew exactly where to lead us next. Fate was guiding our path, confirming that this mistletoe magic, this journey into the heart of Serenity Falls's hidden love stories, was indeed my destiny.

Edna continued, her voice tinged with warmth. "I remember one afternoon, we were discussing the project in the library. Harold was explaining his interpretation of a poem, and it was like watching someone step out of a shadow. He spoke with such passion, it was almost as if he was sharing a piece of his soul. That's the day I truly met Harold Jenkins."

I found myself lost in her narrative, imagining a young Harold, animated and vibrant in a way the man I knew now rarely showed.

Ethan's presence beside me was a grounding force, his interest in the story as keen as mine.

Edna excused herself and returned with an old photo album, its cover worn from years of handling. She began flipping through its pages, each one a portal to the past. The photos ranged from candid schoolyard shots to more formal black and white portraits, each capturing moments of a bygone era.

As she flipped through the album, Ethan and I huddled closer, our shoulders brushing in a way that felt both natural and charged with something unspoken.

"Now this was the winter formal," Edna said, tapping a photo of a group of teenagers lined up in front of a tinsel-draped gymnasium. "That's me there, in the green dress."

Ethan and I leaned in, our heads nearly touching as we squinted at the image. I could feel the warmth of his arm against mine, the slow and steady rhythm of his breathing somehow matching my own. With each turn of the page, we edged a little closer, our thighs bumping gently now and then, sending flickers of awareness through me like sparks leaping from a fire.

"There," Edna said softly, pointing to a smaller photo tucked into the corner of the page. "That was my junior year. I was sixteen."

I followed her finger to the image and stilled. A young, luminous, and utterly open-faced Edna looked out from the black-and-white photo. Her smile was wide, her eyes full of life.

But something didn't align. As I reached out to examine it more closely, mine and Ethan's hands briefly overlapped, lingering just a moment longer than necessary.

I shook off my disorientation at Ethan's touch and studied the photo. A growing sense of disappointment crept in. The girl in this picture, though undoubtedly Edna, was not the one I had seen in Harold's memory. This Edna had neatly coiffed hair, perfectly styled in a fashion of the era, and her features were more reserved and composed. She wore a modest dress and her smile, though pleasant, was controlled, lacking the spontaneous joy of the girl in Harold's recollection.

In contrast, the girl in Harold's memory had a wild cascade of curls, untamed and free-flowing. The realization settled heavily in my chest. Edna was not the secret love Harold had been holding onto all these years.

I masked my letdown with a polite smile, flipping through a few more pages while part of me clung to a thread of hope. "Edna, do you mind if I take a closer look at this one?" I asked, indicating the photo of her at sixteen.

"Of course, dear," she replied, passing the album to me.

As I examined the photograph, the details of Harold's memories played back in my mind. The girl he longed for, her smile in the moonlight, was distinct, vivid, and different from Edna's portrayal in these pictures.

I needed to verify this. If not Edna, then who was the girl who had captured Harold's heart so completely? I looked up from the photograph, meeting Edna's expectant gaze. "Edna, if you don't mind me asking, were you and Harold ever... an item?"

Edna's expression softened with a touch of amusement. "Oh, no, dear. We were never romantically involved. Harold was a good friend, but that's as far as it went." She paused, her eyes reflecting a distant past. "There was a girl, though. Someone special in Harold's life. But he never told me who she was."

My interest deepened, and I leaned in, hanging on her every word. Beside me, Ethan mirrored my movement, our shoulders brushing lightly in a shared moment of anticipation. I glanced at him, noticing the intensity in his eyes, a reflection of my own curiosity and eagerness to unravel the mystery.

"Was there ever any hint about who this girl might have been?" Ethan's voice was low, as if respecting the weight of the moment.

Edna shook her head, her gaze distant.

"No, dear. Harold kept that part of his life close to his chest. Then, one day, he stopped talking about her altogether," Edna continued, her tone turning somber. "Something changed in him after that. He became more withdrawn, more sullen. It was as if a part of him had broken. He never dated again, as far as I knew. Whatever happened with that girl, it left a lasting impact on Harold, shaped the man he became."

As I listened, a resolute determination took hold within me. Harold's story, steeped in silence and shadows, needed to be brought to light. I felt a deep, almost personal responsibility to find out what had happened, to understand the truth behind this lost love that had so profoundly altered a man's life.

Chapter Seven

IN THE SOLARIUM

"I love this room so much. It's like stepping into a living snow globe." Jenna wrapped a cozy throw around her shoulders and nestled into a wicker chair in the solarium. The room, bathed in the soft glow of the winter sun, framed the snowy garden outside. "But you, my friend, look like you're carrying the weight of the world. Is it the inn? I know things have been tough lately."

I settled into the chair opposite Jenna. "You could say that," I admitted, gazing out at the snowy scene. "Guests have been sparse, and the bills just keep coming, no matter what. I really thought the renovations would be enough to bring people in, but..." My voice trailed off, lost in the uncertainty of it all.

Jenna's expression softened with understanding. "I'm sorry, Clara. Fireside Manor is such a special place. There must be a way to turn things around."

"I'm working on it. But let's just say, running a B&B is more complicated than I expected." I offered a wry smile. I had pinned so many hopes on those cookies, each one meticulously baked and decorated, believing they could somehow charm guests into my struggling B&B. But two days later, the phones were still quiet and

I felt a bit foolish. Had I really expected a tray of cookies to solve my entrepreneurial woes?

"Don't underestimate your creativity and determination," said Jenna. "You've made Fireside Manor a beautiful place; the right guests will see that too. They just need a nudge in your direction."

"Well, they better get that nudge soon," I said. "The bank has been breathing down my neck, even threatening to send a representative to check on their 'investment.' I've been dodging their calls and letters. Honestly, I was expecting them to crash my Christmas, but it's been eerily quiet. Maybe they've let up for the holidays?"

Jenna raised an eyebrow. "Or maybe they're just regrouping. Banks don't just forget about their loans, Clara."

I sighed, anxiety fluttering in my chest. "I guess I'm just hoping for a little Christmas miracle. Something to shift the energy before they show up with their clipboards and judgments. If only cookies could fix everything."

My gaze drifted to the window, the snowy landscape outside offering a brief, calming pause.

I gave a small, self-deprecating laugh. "My guest would probably have a field day with my failed cookie-marketing plan."

I turned to Jenna and added, "He's in marketing."

Jenna's eyes, always so perceptive, twinkled. "That sounds perfect! You should ask him for help."

"I could never!" I balked at the thought. "It would be far too embarrassing. Anyway, I need to do this myself, if only to prove to myself that I can."

"So, how's it going with our mysterious city dweller?"

The question pulled me back from my internal reflections on failed cookie strategies. "Ethan's off exploring the town, giving me some space to... well, sort through some rather unusual developments." I hesitated, then, with a sigh, launched into the tale of the magical mistletoe kisses and the enigmatic Harold Jenkins. I felt a tinge of relief, sharing something so profoundly outside the realm of everyday worries.

As I told her everything, Jenna shifted in her seat, pulling the blanket tighter around her shoulders. "Clara, you're not seriously saying you can hear people's thoughts under the mistletoe?" she asked, her voice uncertain. "That's... a lot."

"I know how it sounds," I said. "But it's real." I met her eyes, my heart thudding. "And I heard yours, too. About Maggie."

The color drained from her face. "You... you know?"

I nodded. "I do. And honestly? I'm more surprised you never told me. I thought we shared everything."

"We do!" she said quickly, then looked down, twisting the edge of the throw between her fingers. "I just... I didn't know how. I kept thinking it would pass. That it wasn't worth the risk."

"What kind of risk?"

She sighed. "Everything. What if she didn't feel the same? Or worse, what if she did, and it blew up later? I didn't want to break the friend group, didn't want to make things weird. It felt safer to say nothing."

Her voice cracked just a little, and I could hear all the weight behind it.

I reached across the couch and placed my hand over hers. "Jen, your feelings aren't something to be ashamed of. And no matter what happens with Maggie, nothing changes us."

She looked up at me, eyes shining with a mix of gratitude and uncertainty. "Thanks, Clara. I just... she's gone now. And things are complicated."

I gave her hand a gentle squeeze. "I get it. Just... whenever you're ready to talk about it, I'm here."

Jenna smiled softly. Then, her expression turned playful. "Speaking of love stories, what about you and Ethan? That kiss at the festival has set the town abuzz. There's clearly more than just investigative curiosity there."

My cheeks flushed at the mention of Ethan. "Oh, that? It was part of my... research," I stammered, avoiding her gaze.

"Uh-huh, sure." Jenna was clearly not convinced. "Come on, Clara. There's some magic there, and I'm not just talking about the mistletoe. You can't hide it from me."

I exhaled, nerves twisting in my chest. There was apprehension, yes, but something else, too. Something unfamiliar and quietly hopeful.

"There might be something," I said, the words catching on the edge of my breath. Saying it out loud felt like betraying all the walls I'd carefully built.

"But I'm not going to chase it."

Jenna studied me, her eyes reflecting a deep understanding of the unspoken fears behind my words. "Clara, just because you've had relationship troubles in the past doesn't mean every hello leads to heartbreak. I know your last breakup was bad. You hardly ever talk about it."

"Julian chose a different path. One that didn't include me." The memory flooded back—Julian, his hesitant voice the night before our wedding, telling me he couldn't go through with it. That he'd met someone else. I remembered looking down at the engagement ring on my finger, feeling as if the ground had vanished beneath me.

I pulled myself back to the present. "And yeah, it stings. Now, I find myself more comfortable with the brief hellos and goodbyes of guests than the idea of someone sticking around for the long haul." I attempted a shrug, coating my confession with a layer of humor to mask the rawness of the wound.

Jenna's hand, warm and reassuring, found mine. "Ethan isn't Julian. You deserve to give love a second chance."

I shook my head. "Julian was me giving love a *third* chance. They always say third time's the charm. Well, my charm is clearly broken."

Yet her words sent ripples of 'what-ifs' and 'maybes' through my mind. I found myself lost in the dance of the snowflakes outside the window, each following its own unique trajectory. And in that moment, I wondered if perhaps my story was poised to turn a new page—a chapter not shadowed by the past but illuminated by the potential of what lay ahead.

Jenna's eyes sparkled as she observed my contemplation. "You know, there's something hilariously ironic about this whole situation. Clara Winters, the self-proclaimed cynic of soulmates, now bidden by mistletoe magic to play matchmaker for the town curmudgeon, of all people. It's like fate has a sense of humor."

I couldn't help but let out a reluctant chuckle, even as I shook my head. "Oh, please, Jenna. Soulmates? That's just a fanciful notion for fairy tales and romance novels. I'm just stumbling through a strange twist of fate, that's all."

"But Clara, considering everything that's happened, don't you think maybe—just maybe—there's something to this soulmate business? Even a tiny bit?"

I sighed, looking back out at the snowflakes, each so distinct. "Soulmates are a fantasy, Jenna. People are just people, with their own quirks and stories. They come and go, like guests at the inn."

Jenna gave me a knowing look, as if she saw right through my defenses. "We'll see, Clara. We'll see. Just remember, every snowflake finds its place in the grand design, even if it takes a little dance in the wind to get there."

CHAPTER EIGHT

STANDOFF AT THE LIBRARY

I was three chapters deep into *Charm & Profit: Reimagining Your B&B for Today's Traveler* and still no closer to saving Fireside Manor from financial ruin.

"Sell the experience," the book advised. "Craft a story. Lean into the nostalgia."

Great. Maybe I could charge extra for existential dread and creaky floorboards.

The Serenity Falls Library was quiet as ever, the kind of quiet that made your thoughts echo. I sat tucked between the towering shelves of the marketing section, equal parts desperate and hopeful.

The town clock chimed noon, loud enough to make me jump. I hadn't even realized the morning had slipped away. Time was moving faster than my progress—and it wasn't just the inn's future that had me on edge.

Because I definitely wasn't thinking about Ethan.

Not about his ridiculous smile. Not about how he actually listened when I talked. And absolutely not about the way his presence had started to feel comfortable. Dangerous.

As I made my way to the checkout, my footsteps echoed on the polished wooden floor. The grand architecture of the library enveloped me. High ceilings adorned with intricate moldings loomed above, and the scent of aged books filled the air, a familiar and comforting aroma.

It was then that a movement in the archives section caught my eye.

It was Ethan, his attention absorbed by a pile of old documents and photographs spread before him. The sight of him, so engrossed in his research amidst the ancient tomes and the library's whispered stories, captivated me more than I cared to admit. There was something about the way he leaned over the table, his brows furrowed in concentration, that drew me in, and I found myself pausing, appreciating the scene before me.

But what was he doing rummaging through the archives? Surely he wasn't researching Harold Jenkins without me. After all, this is my town. *My* curmudgeon. I was the one with the mistletoe magic!

I didn't realize I'd been staring until his eyes met mine. Startled, like a cat caught atop a forbidden bookshelf, he quickly smoothed his expression into that familiar, easy smile that always seemed to know more than it let on.

Feeling a sudden self-consciousness of my own, I hastily slid the book behind my back. The last thing I wanted was for Ethan, one of the few guests keeping my B&B afloat, to see the extent of my concerns about the business.

I approached, trying to sound casual, though my heart beat a little faster at the sight of him. "Fancy seeing you here. Diving into Serenity Falls's history?"

"Just satisfying some curiosity about this town." His eyes flickered to the book I was awkwardly hiding.

I shifted the book further behind me, feeling a bit like a child caught with her hand in the cookie jar. "And what specific part of our history has caught your interest?" I asked, hoping to steer the conversation away from my hidden book. And figure out what the heck he was doing here.

Ethan shuffled the papers in front of him. "Oh, you know, just getting a feel for the place." His eyes briefly darted away before meeting mine again. He tapped a finger on an old photograph as if to underscore his casual interest. "Every town has its stories, right?"

His smile was easy, but there was a tightness around his eyes that suggested he wasn't sharing the whole story.

In response, I arched an eyebrow, allowing it to slowly climb higher on my forehead. My gaze remained fixed on Ethan, a playful glint in my eye that I hoped broadcasted my skepticism. I let the corner of my mouth quirk up in a half-smile, as if to say, *Really now, is that the best you've got?*

We were engaged in what could only be described as the world's most awkward standoff. I clutched *Charm & Profit* behind my back like a butt shield, while Ethan hovered over the archives like a detective with too many clues. We exchanged stares, each clearly holding onto our little mysteries. Two spies unsure if they were on the same mission. The silence stretched on, filled with unvoiced questions, as if we were each waiting for the other to blink first in this impromptu game of investigative hide-and-seek.

Ethan's gaze lingered on the space behind me, a hint of curiosity in his eyes. "Hiding a steamy romance back there?"

His words, the light-hearted jest in his tone, struck a chord within me. Ethan had been nothing but kind and helpful, a stark contrast to... well. Yet here he was, willingly spending his vacation on what could only be described as a whimsical, if not outright bizarre, mission.

And then my rebellious mind went to my first boyfriend. Alex. The thought of my ex joining me on such an endeavor was almost laughable. I could almost hear his derisive chuckle if I'd ever mentioned something as whimsical as magical mistletoe powers. "Really, Clara? Next, you'll be telling me you're moonlighting as a fairy godmother," he'd probably say, voice dripping with sarcasm. Alex and I had shared many things, but a belief in the enchanting, the unexplainable? That was a bridge too weird for him to cross.

Ethan, on the other hand, had not only crossed that bridge but seemed to be strolling along it with an open mind and a heart willing to embrace the unknown. It was refreshing. And a bit disarming.

And here I was, hiding things from him. The same way my third love, Julian, had hid things from me. I had vowed never to do that to someone.

The absurdity of the situation, the strain of keeping the inn afloat, the burden of untold stories, it all felt overwhelming. Like a dam giving way, something inside me cracked, the facade of composure I'd been desperately holding onto crumbling away.

I brought the book into view, stifling a grimace. "Fireside Manor isn't exactly flourishing these days. I'm scouring for any advice that might keep the ship from sinking."

As the words tumbled out, part of me couldn't believe I was sharing my financial woes with Ethan, a guest and practically a stranger. Yet, there was something about him—perhaps his earnest demeanor or the way he listened—that made it feel less daunting to reveal the cracks in my carefully maintained facade.

Ethan's expression softened, a blend of empathy and concern replacing his earlier amusement. "I had no idea you were facing such challenges," he said. "Running a place like Fireside Manor, it must be quite the undertaking, especially in these times. I'm here if you ever want to talk about it."

I nodded, a bittersweet smile touching my lips. It felt strangely liberating to acknowledge the struggles out loud, even as a part of me braced for judgment or pity. But Ethan offered neither—just sincere support and a willing ear.

It was comforting, unexpectedly so, to have someone listen with-out offering quick fixes or empty platitudes. In Ethan's simple offer of support, I found a glimmer of solace, and a reminder that some-times, the act of sharing one's struggles can be as healing as finding their solutions.

Just as I began to feel a semblance of comfort in sharing my plight with Ethan, the familiar, inquisitive voice of Doris Fletcher echoed through the archives. "Aha! Caught in the act of... historical research?" she declared with her usual flair for the dramatic entrance.

Doris was wrapped in a vibrant, patchwork quilted jacket that seemed to have lived through as many winters as she had, each pattern a story in itself. A cozy, woolen scarf, knitted in a riot of colors that only Doris could pull off, completed her ensemble. She approached us with an impish glint in her eye. Her gaze darted between me, Ethan, and the tell-tale book in my hands.

"Clara, my dear, and Mr. Mysterious City Slicker," she greeted, her voice bubbling with the excitement of a child in a candy store. "What an unexpected pair you make amidst these archives. Digging up dirt or just dust?"

Ethan, with the grace of someone used to navigating social land-mines, flashed Doris a charmingly disarming smile. "Merely appre-ciating the rich history of Serenity Falls." A quick, knowing look passed between us.

Doris, however, zeroed in on my book with the accuracy of a heat-seeking missile. "Oh, Clara, is everything alright with the B&B? I just happened to notice your parking lot's been rather empty late-ly," she remarked, her tone teetering between genuine concern and an eagerness to be in the know.

Her knack for observing and commenting on the smallest de-tails of town life was as sharp as ever—a fact that was particularly impressive, or perhaps intrusive, considering the B&B's remote and secluded location. The woman had never set foot on the property, yet her awareness of its emptiness was uncanny. Perhaps she had a network of informants reporting back on the comings and goings in Serenity Falls. The thought was amusing and unnerving in equal measure.

I flashed what I hoped was a convincingly casual smile. "Just broadening my horizons, Doris. You know me, always a student at heart."

To my surprise, Doris responded with a knowing nod that carried an unexpected warmth. Her eyes, often sharp with the thrill of unearthing town secrets, softened as they met mine. It was a look that, in that brief moment, seemed to say, *we all have our struggles, dear.* Her response, unexpectedly kind, offered a small comfort, a brief respite from the relentless pressure of keeping up appearances.

And then Doris launched into the latest gossip.

I shared a look with Ethan that said, *get us out of here!*

To my complete dismay, however, Ethan seemed more intrigued by Doris's presence than eager to leave.

"Ms. Fletcher, what brings you to the archives today?" he asked, with what appeared to be genuine interest.

Doris hesitated for a fraction of a second, "Oh, no I'm not here for the archives at all! I actually came to check out some records."

Ethan's interest visibly piqued at the mention of records. "Vinyls, you mean?"

She nodded.

"I've always had a soft spot for vintage music," he said. "I never imagined this library would have vinyls available for checkout."

Doris's face brightened like she'd just found a long-lost friend. "Well, those are my doing. I've been collecting records since I was a girl. My favorite are the polkas. There's nothing like a good polka to lift your spirits. I wanted to spread that joy, so I donated my collection here. It's like having my own personal jukebox. I just come and check them out whenever I need a fix."

Ethan lit up. "I grew up listening to polka music! It's a bit of a rare interest these days."

I nearly choked. Polka? Seriously?

In seconds, he and Doris were swapping stories about polka bands and accordion legends like long-lost cousins at a family reunion. Their voices rose with enthusiasm, echoing through the archives like a particularly cheerful fever dream.

I hovered awkwardly nearby, caught between secondhand embarrassment and reluctant amusement. Somehow, I'd gone from dodging Doris's nosiness to watching Ethan charm her with polka trivia. Polka. Of all things.

It was moments like these that made me wonder if my life had always been this odd, or if Ethan had brought a new level of peculiarity to my days.

"Since you're such a fan..." Doris began rummaging through her purse with the eagerness of a magician pulling out a trick, then finally produced a flyer adorned with colorful illustrations of dancing couples and festive decorations. "You simply must come to our Christmas Eve polka bash." She waved the flyer like a flag of victory. "It's the highlight of Serenity Falls's holiday season, and I insist you don't miss it. And bring Clara along, dear, she could use a bit of festive cheer!"

I raised an eyebrow, watching the scene unfold. The thought of a Christmas Eve polka bash was amusing and terrifying. Ethan, however, seemed genuinely intrigued, accepting the flyer with an enthusiastic nod. "It sounds like a unique experience, Doris. Thank you."

Doris, seemingly satisfied with her successful recruitment, tucked her purse under her arm. "Wonderful! It's a date then. Well, not a date-date, unless you two..." she trailed off, her eyes twinkling with unspoken suggestions.

I interjected, grasping at the first excuse that came to mind. "We'll see, Doris. Actually, Ethan and I have a lunch date we need to get to." The words were out before I could even consider their implications. *A lunch date? Really, Clara?*

Doris, however, seemed delighted by this development. "Oh, how lovely! Don't let me keep you, then. Enjoy your lunch!" She waved us off with a flourish.

I gently tugged at Ethan's arm, leading him away from the archives. "Sorry about that, but I figured it was our best escape route," I said, trying to sound casual.

Ethan, following along as we left the library, wore a teasing grin. "A lunch date, eh? I wasn't aware we had such plans, but I must say, I'm intrigued."

"Well, I'm full of surprises. Besides, it's not a bad idea, grabbing some lunch. We can discuss our... what should I call it... our polka predicament?"

"I see no predicament. But sure. Lunch sounds good."

Walking side by side, I found myself amused by the unexpected twists of the day. With Ethan, even a simple lunch seemed to promise its own set of adventures. Serenity Falls was a town of surprises, and Ethan, it appeared, was keen on keeping that tradition alive.

Chapter Nine

THE IVY NOOK

"So, what's the grand plan with your new library treasure?" Ethan's voice, playful and light, wove seamlessly into the soft jazz melody drifting through The Ivy Nook. Around us, the restaurant basked in a lazy winter sunbeam, casting a warm, amber hue over the scattered tables and their occupants, lost in hushed conversations and solitary musings.

Before I could answer, Sophia, our ever-energetic waitress, bounced over to our table. She was a whirlwind of cheer, her dark ponytail bobbing with each step. With a flourish, she placed Ethan's club sandwich, its layers looking like a mini culinary skyscraper, in front of him and set down my tomato bisque with a theatrical bow. The soup's aroma promised a warm, herb-infused embrace. "Here you go, folks! Enjoy your lunch," she announced with a zest that was as infectious as her smile.

Sophia turned to me. "And Clara, I'll be seeing you at tomorrow's book club, right? We're all dying to hear your take on *The Midnight Library*."

"Wouldn't miss it for the world." I replied, returning her smile.

Sophia zipped away, her ponytail a cheerful flag waving behind her. She glanced back, covertly giving me the thumbs-up as she sized up Ethan with a gawk of approval. I suppressed a laugh. *Well, at least someone's optimistic about my love life.*

Sometimes, I wished I could bottle up Sophia's energy, a sunbeam in human form. Still in the throes of her college years, majoring in English, she was the youngest—and the most enthusiastic—member of our book club. Her insights, often peppered with youthful exuberance and literary fervor, brought a refreshing vibrancy to our discussions.

I turned back to my date (was this a date?). Sharing this moment with Ethan in the cozy embrace of The Ivy Nook, my little haven, felt unexpectedly special. The restaurant, with its ivy-laced walls and soft, golden light, had always been a spot where time seemed to pause, allowing for the small, beautiful details of life to come into sharper focus. Here, among the familiar faces and the comforting scents of home-cooked meals, even the most ordinary day gained a hint of enchantment.

"Now, about that library treasure," I said, shifting gears. "Honestly, I'm not sure a book can save Fireside Manor at this point."

Ethan leaned in, elbows on the table. "I don't usually hand out unsolicited advice, but... I *do* help businesses with their marketing strategies. If you want, I could take a look. Offer a few ideas?"

I smoothed the edge of my napkin, suddenly very focused on the weave of the fabric.

He caught himself. "Only if you're up for it. I don't want to overstep."

Ethan raised his eyebrows, then smiled—one of those slow, eye-crinkling smiles that sent a small, inconvenient flutter through my chest. "Hope and caffeine, huh? That's a foundation. Let's build on it. I promise, I'll go easy on you."

"You're serious about this?" I asked, caught off guard by the warmth in his eyes. "I mean, I appreciate it, but I'd hate to impose.

Marketing a small-town B&B is probably a far cry from whatever big-city accounts you usually handle."

"It's no imposition," he said without hesitation. "Sometimes an outside perspective is exactly what you need. And who knows, Fireside Manor might be sitting on untapped potential."

It was tempting. Really tempting. And terrifying. Letting someone peek behind the curtain, see just how close I was to losing everything? That wasn't easy. But Ethan's sincerity chipped away at my resolve.

Still. I needed to prove I could handle this on my own.

"Thanks," I said. "I'll think about it."

He nodded and took another bite of his sandwich, leaving the offer hanging between us, full of possibility.

The room suddenly felt smaller. Closer. More personal.

"So, this big-city marketing life of yours..." I hesitated, stabbing at my soup like it might rescue me. "Any, uh—wife? Girlfriend? Boyfriend? All of the above?"

Oh no. Abort. Back up, Clara. Not that intimate.

He paused, sandwich halfway to his mouth. A flicker of surprise crossed his face, then he grinned. "No wife, no girlfriend, no boyfriend. Just me and a very demanding houseplant that's definitely judging my erratic sleep schedule."

I laughed, tension slipping from my shoulders. "A judgmental houseplant, huh? Sounds like a serious commitment."

He nodded, mock-serious. "Oh, it's a relationship built on mutual deception—I pretend to know what I'm doing, and it pretends to thrive."

"Sounds like a solid foundation. Truly symbiotic."

Ethan dabbed his lips with a napkin. "So, any significant... houseplants in your life?"

I nearly snorted into my coffee. "Houseplants? Please. They fear me. But there *is* a rolling pin in my life that holds some serious status."

His eyes widened just slightly. I saw the blush bloom across his cheeks right as I realized how that sounded.

"For baking!" I added quickly. "Obviously. Baking."

His blush deepened, but his laugh was rich and easy. "Of course. For baking. I wouldn't dare assume otherwise."

"Actually," I said, the humor softening into something more honest, "I haven't really dated anyone since... well, since Julian."

Ethan's expression softened, an unspoken invitation to continue. I found myself opening up, the words flowing more easily than I expected. "Julian and I were engaged. He broke it off the night before our wedding. It's been two years now."

The memory of that night with Julian unfolded in my mind like a vivid, unwelcome horror film. I remembered the dim lighting of our living room, casting long shadows as he stood there, a man torn apart by his own indecision. The look of deep regret in his eyes was etched in my memory, a haunting mix of sorrow and resignation.

"I can't do this, Clara. I'm sorry," Julian had said, his voice faltering, breaking the silence that hung heavy in the air. His words reverberated through the room, each syllable a hammer to my heart.

Around us, the last-minute details of our wedding preparations—the floral arrangements awaiting their final touches, the beautiful place cards not yet set at each table, the elegant wedding gown hanging in its garment bag—all seemed to mock the fragility of our plans. I could still smell the faint, sweet scent of roses and lilies, intertwined in the air, a bitter reminder of a celebration that would never happen.

I'd stood there, frozen, the chill of the room seeping into my bones. My hands trembled, barely able to grasp the reality that was crumbling before me. The pain was sharp and immediate, a physical ache that mirrored the emotional turmoil inside.

In that moment, the future I had envisioned with Julian had shattered into a thousand unrecognizable pieces. The life I thought I wanted, the love I believed was mine—all of it dissolved in the wake of his words.

Gradually, the restaurant came back into focus, pulling me from the grip of the past. Ethan's voice, warm and understanding, reached me from across the table. "I'm sorry to hear that, Clara. That must have been tough." His reaction was a perfect blend of sympathy and respect, no pity or awkwardness.

I shrugged, a bittersweet smile playing on my lips. "It was. But it also taught me a lot. About myself, about what I want... and what I don't."

There was a moment of comfortable silence between us, a shared understanding that some experiences, however painful, shape us in ways we never expect. It was the first time I had spoken about Julian without feeling a weight on my chest, and it surprised me how much lighter I felt.

Ethan reached across the table, his gesture offering silent support. "It sounds like you've come a long way since then."

I nodded. "I have. After things ended with Julian, I needed a fresh start, something to call my own. That's when I bought Fireside Manor. It's been more than just a business to me; it's been a place of healing, a new beginning."

As we wrapped up our meal, Sophia breezed back to our table. With a swift, practiced motion, she gathered our plates. "How was everything?" she beamed.

"It was absolutely delicious, thanks," I responded, charmed by her buoyancy.

Her eyes lit up. "And for dessert? Have you tried our apple crumble? It's like a hug in a bowl!"

Ethan gave the dessert menu a cursory glance, then turned to me with an inquisitive raise of his eyebrow. "What do you think? Shall we?"

I found myself swept up in the moment. "Why not? The apple crumble sounds perfect."

"Make that two," said Ethan, closing the menu.

Sophia's grin widened. "You're in for a treat."

After she left, Ethan turned his attention back to me, his expression shifting to a more reflective tone. "It's really wonderful how Fireside Manor has been such a place of healing for you." he said, his voice tinged with a note of wistfulness. "I understand the need for a new beginning. I... I've been looking for a change myself, especially after...well, after my father passed away recently."

His words lingered between us, reflecting a mutual understanding of loss and the need to fill the emptiness it leaves behind. "I'm sorry for your loss."

"Thank you, Clara." He gave a small, appreciative smile. "It's been hard, dealing with grief and the estate. It made me realize how much I needed a break from the city, from the life I was leading. That's what brought me to Serenity Falls—this quest for something different, something meaningful."

The soft jazz melody blended with the murmur of conversations around us. I looked across the table at Ethan, feeling a tug of curiosity. "Were you close with your father?"

For a moment, Ethan's expression closed off, as if he was walking through a memory he wasn't sure he wanted to revisit. Then, slowly, his features softened, and he met my gaze with a vulnerability that hadn't been there before. "We were close... in a complicated way."

I nodded, giving him the space to continue, aware of the delicate territory we were venturing into.

He took a deep breath, and when he spoke again, his voice was reflective. "My dad was a man of powerful influence. Sometimes too strong. We didn't always see eye to eye, especially when I chose a career in marketing over joining the family business."

"Families can be... challenging," I said.

Sophia returned, deftly balancing a large plate in her hand. With a flourish, she set down two coffees and a single, generously-sized apple crumble in the center of our table, along with two spoons. "I am so sorry, it looks like this was the last one."

She didn't sound sorry at all.

"But I bet it's more fun to share, right?" she said with a wink.

There was a moment of hesitation as Ethan and I exchanged a glance, an unspoken question hanging in the air. The warmth of the situation flushed my cheeks.

"Looks like we've got no choice," said Ethan, his voice low and tinged with a playful note. He picked up one spoon and gestured for me to do the same.

I rolled my eyes playfully, a mock sigh escaping my lips. *Sophia, you're on my hit list at next week's book club.*

We both leaned in over the apple crumble, our proximity so close I could feel the warmth of Ethan's breath. The scent of baked apples and cinnamon wove through the moment, adding a sweet, spiced layer to our closeness.

With each spoonful, the space between us seemed to shrink, filled with an unspoken tension, our eyes occasionally meeting and then darting away. The dessert seemed to last an eternity, yet ended too soon. I savored not just the crumble, but the nearness of Ethan, a sensation both thrilling and unnerving.

As the crumble dwindled, Ethan paused, leaving one final bite on the plate. He set his spoon down, upside down, as if officially retiring from the dessert dance. "This reminds me a bit of my dad," he said. "Every autumn, we would go apple picking. It was our tradition. He'd let me climb the ladders and choose any apple I wanted, no matter how high or hidden it was."

I could almost see the orchard in my mind, the trees heavy with fruit under a crisp fall sky. "That sounds wonderful," I said, while also eyeing the last bite of apple crumble, then at Ethan's upside-down spoon. Was this a chivalrous gesture, leaving the last bite for me? Should I wait a bit before going in for the last bite? What's the shared-dessert protocol here?

"It was," he agreed, his smile growing warmer. "He used to say, 'It's not about finding the perfect apples, but about finding the perfect moments.' I think he was teaching me to appreciate the journey, not just the destination."

"What a beautiful lesson." I felt a newfound warmth for this man who was revealing the layers of his life to me.

Ethan nodded, his gaze returning to the present. "Yeah, it was. I miss him. His lessons, his stubbornness, even his terrible jokes."

I reached out, my hand lightly touching his. "Thank you for sharing that with me."

He turned his hand under mine, giving it a gentle squeeze. "Thank you for listening."

With a wry smile, I scooped up the final piece of crumble. "You know, it's funny," I mused, savoring the sweetness, "how life throws us these curveballs. One minute you're enjoying apple crumble, the next, you're pondering deep life lessons over the last bite."

Ethan leaned back in his chair, his gaze locking with mine. "Yeah, sometimes those curveballs lead us to unexpected places. Or people." His eyes crinkled with a hint of mischief.

I laughed, the sound mingling with the gentle clinking of dishes and the low hum of conversation in the background of the restaurant. "Well, I never thought I'd be running a bed and breakfast in a small town, much less pairing up with a stranger to search for the town curmudgeon's high school sweetheart."

He raised an eyebrow, his smile broadening. "Stranger, huh? I was hoping we were past that by now."

"Oh, I don't know," I said, "I might need an epic saga detailing every single moment of your life—complete with plot twists, a dramatic soundtrack, and maybe a cameo by a famous actor—before I can officially upgrade your status."

"Wait until you hear about the time I heroically saved a kitten from a tree." Ethan's smile played at the corners of his mouth in a mischievous way that was becoming familiar.

Sophia came by and refilled our mugs. The conversation shifted gears as Ethan delved into stories from his travels. He spoke of hiking in the Andes, navigating the chaotic streets of Bangkok, and his impromptu salsa dancing lessons in Cuba. His enthusiasm was contagious, and I found myself leaning in, completely captivated. It wasn't just the adventures themselves that held my attention, but the way his eyes sparkled with life when he recounted them, the animated gestures of his hands painting pictures in the air, the warmth and vibrancy in his voice. Each story was a window into a world of experiences, and I felt myself drawn into them, eager for more.

At some point, our conversation drifted away from travels, meandering through tales of our childhoods, our dreams, and even a debate over the best holiday movies. Time seemed to slip away unnoticed, our laughter and shared stories filling the space. As we talked, I noticed my heart beating a bit faster, a sensation I hadn't felt for two years. More, if I were being honest with myself. There was something about Ethan that felt comforting, yet excitingly fresh. It showed in how he listened, genuinely attentive to my words, and in how openly he shared his own vulnerabilities.

I was in the midst of arguing the superior comedic timing in *Elf* when Sophia reappeared at our table. "Okay, folks, I hate to play the party pooper, but we're about to close up for our afternoon break."

I looked around, startled to see empty chairs and elongated shadows cast by the shifting winter sun. "Really? Have we been chatting for that long?"

Sophia nodded, her eyes twinkling with mirth. "Yep, you two have been at it for three hours straight. I think you've set a new Ivy Nook record for the longest date."

I raised my eyebrows dramatically. "Date? Sophia, we've been deeply engrossed in... uh, discussing the critical intricacies of... well, you know, very serious things."

Sophia narrowed her eyes, clearly not buying my feeble cover-up. "Of course, the most serious matters. Well, your 'critical discussion' will have to continue elsewhere. We've got to prep for the dinner rush."

Ethan and I exchanged a look, a mix of amusement and a hint of reluctance to end our time together.

"How about we adjourn to Fireside Manor?" asked Ethan as we gathered our things. "Seems like the perfect spot to continue our... business discussions."

"That sounds like a plan. Plus, I can make us some hot cocoa. It's kind of a specialty of mine." I was already picturing the cozy setting of my B&B.

Ethan adopted a mock-serious tone. "And for our next agenda item at Fireside Manor, I present The Toasted Bread Experience. Brace yourself for the culinary marvel of my unparalleled butter-to-bread ratio."

"Do you really think you're ready to pit your toast against Tom's elderberry swirl pastries?"

"Oh, Clara." Ethan draped an arm around my shoulder. "I was born ready."

I led the way to Fireside Manor with a playful roll of my eyes. Our footsteps crunched softly on the path. The rest of the short walk was filled with the kind of light-hearted banter that comes easily when two people are just starting to discover the rhythms of each other's humor.

As the night unfolded, with hot cocoa—and toast—in hand, our conversation meandered through topics both light and profound. Soon, the fire in the hearth dwindled to a soft glow, casting a warm, golden light over us. I found myself reluctant to end the night, to break the spell that had enveloped us. Ethan seemed to sense it too, his gaze lingering on me a moment longer than necessary.

Finally, he stood up, stretching his arms. "I should probably let you get some rest," he said, though his voice held a hint of reluctance.

I walked him to his door, the wooden floorboards creaking beneath our feet. "Thank you, Ethan, for everything today. It's been... more than I expected." Then I cleared my throat, putting on my hostess hat. "And if you need anything—extra towels, soap, proton pack—just text me."

He turned to face me, his hand resting lightly on the doorknob. "Clara, I—" He paused, the words hanging in the air. Then, as if making a decision, he stepped closer, his gaze intensifying. "Actually, there is something."

Before I could form words, Ethan bridged the gap between us. His eyes, deep pools of earnest curiosity, held mine in a gaze that felt like it was unraveling the layers of my heart. There was a question in his eyes, a silent asking for permission that sent a warmth through my chest.

As he leaned in, the verdant scent of his cologne mixed with the smoky remnants of our evening by the fire. His hand, tentative yet sure, found its way to the small of my back, pulling me closer. I could feel the warmth of his breath just moments before his lips met mine.

His kiss was soft, a gentle exploration that coaxed my lips open. The slight pressure of his hand on my lower back, the brush of his thumb against the fabric of my shirt, sent a cascade of sensations rippling through me. The world around us—the creaking of the floorboards, the distant hush of the wind outside—melted away. All that existed in that suspended moment was the soft press of his lips, the faint rustle of fabric as we moved closer, and the reassuring warmth of his body pressed against mine.

And then he pulled away. "Goodnight, Clara," he whispered, his smile reflecting the same wonder I felt.

"Goodnight, Ethan," I replied, watching him disappear through the door, my heart fluttering with a newfound hope.

I leaned against the now-closed door, a smile spreading across my face. For the first time in a long time, I allowed myself to embrace the excitement and uncertainty of what lay ahead.

Chapter Ten

BOOK CLUB

By the time I pulled up to Jenna's house, the last streaks of sunset had faded into twilight, and her windows glowed like little beacons in the December dark. Book club night was one of the only things that could lure me away from Ethan and the lingering fizz of that fantastic kiss. Because now, I got to go gossip about said kiss.

I smiled to myself, thinking of Ethan back at the B&B, probably toasting something ridiculous to go with the charcuterie board I'd left him for dinner.

Jenna's house, as always, looked like it had been styled by a very enthusiastic artist with access to a glitter gun. Hand-painted ornaments dangled from the bare porch tree, catching the porch light like stained glass. I remembered when she helped me repaint my sitting room, smudged with yellow paint and declaring, *It's all about seeing the potential,* like she was conjuring beauty with a brush.

She probably *could* turn a toothpick and some string into a masterpiece.

Before I could knock, the front door swung open.

"Clara! Always the first to arrive," Jenna beamed, already reaching for the charcuterie tray in my hands. She waved me in.

The entryway was a gallery of colors and shapes. Walls adorned with abstract paintings pulsed with vibrant hues, while sculptures of twisted metal and glass caught the light in a display of shadows and brilliance.

"Your house is like stepping into a daydream," I remarked, hanging my coat on a stand that was an imaginative concoction of vintage umbrella handles.

Jenna's laughter filled the entryway. She gestured towards the living room, where a delightful hodgepodge of mismatched chairs and cushions awaited. "It's easy when I have friends who see the magic in the mundane."

I followed Jenna into the living room and settled into an armchair, its fluffiness rivaling that of a cloud, while Jenna set the charcuterie tray on the coffee table and handed me a glass of wine.

"Thanks," I said, fingers curling around the stem.

My gaze drifted to the mantel, where a photograph of last year's Christmas party caught my eye. Jenna, Maggie, Sophia, and me, crammed together in front of the tree, cheeks flushed from mulled wine and laughter. In the photo, Jenna and Maggie had their arms slung around each other, and the way Jenna was looking at her... it was so full of adoration, I couldn't believe I'd ever missed it.

Jenna followed my gaze, then sank onto the couch across from me. She ran her finger along the rim of her wine glass, thoughtful. "It's been tough trying to find someone who can fill Maggie's shoes."

I glanced over, raising an eyebrow. "In the book club, or in your life?"

She gave a quiet laugh, brushing a strand of hair behind her ear. "Maggie brought a unique energy, didn't she? Our discussions haven't been quite the same since she moved away."

I wrapped both hands around my glass, letting its warmth settle over me. "True. But we've managed to keep the spirit alive. Who knew replacing a Maggie would be such a tall order?"

Jenna sighed and set her glass down with a soft clink. "We certainly set the bar pretty high with her."

That or we had some really bad luck at finding a replacement. First there was Harriet, the one-track mind, who had an uncanny ability to connect every storyline back to ancient Roman history, regardless of the book's actual subject. Then there was Laura, the quintessential contrarian. Regardless of the book or general consensus, she always took an opposing view, apparently just for the sake of argument. But perhaps the most challenging had been Eleanor, the dominator. Her thunderous voice and strong opinions often overshadowed the rest of the group.

"Hopefully this guest Sophia's bringing will be just what we are looking for," I said.

The sound of the doorbell signaled new arrivals. Sophia burst in, her usual effervescent self, holding a tray of cookies and accompanied by a woman with a distinct literary aura about her, the kind that screamed 'I've read every obscure poet you've never heard of and probably attend underground poetry slams for fun.' She wore a black turtleneck, and her eyes had the far-off gaze of someone perpetually lost in thought.

"Everyone, this is Eliza," said Sophia with a flourish. "She's in my creative writing class. Thought she'd enjoy our little bookish soirée."

Eliza extended a hand adorned with multiple silver rings, her handshake firm, her smile enigmatic. "Pleased to meet you all."

"Welcome," I said. "Join us in the hallowed halls of literary debate, where we solemnly swear to take books more seriously than life itself."

A mild scoff escaped Eliza's lips. "Ah, well, I do hope the discussions here transcend the boundaries of the common bookshelf."

Well, dang. Another dud.

Jenna gestured to a chair. "You'll find we take a rather eclectic approach to literature here. A bit of everything, from the classics to the unconventional."

Sophia and I busied ourselves arranging an assortment of snacks on the coffee table, while Jenna handled the wine pouring duties. This evening, the spotlight was on Matt Haig's *The Midnight Library*, a novel that had captivated my imagination.

As we settled in, the conversation gravitated toward the book. *The Midnight Library* was an intriguing exploration about the choices we make and the lives we could have led. Weaving between alternate realities based on different decisions, the narrative had left me pondering my own what-ifs.

Jenna, wine glass in hand, said. "This book really makes you think, doesn't it? About all those crossroads in life, each leading to a different destiny."

Eliza adjusted her beret with the seriousness of a general strategizing a battle. "Indeed. It's a compelling meditation on the nature of regret and happiness. The idea that somewhere exists a life where we made the 'right' choices is both fascinating and haunting."

Nibbling on a cracker, I considered her words. "But isn't there something freeing about that? The notion that there isn't just one perfect path, but many different ones, each with its unique set of highs and lows?"

"There is," added Sophia. "It's fascinating to think about all the different lives we could lead. Which book among those endless green shelves we would choose."

Eliza, with a thoughtful expression, swirled the wine in her glass. "I think I'd be a world-traveling journalist, chasing stories in exotic locales, living out of a suitcase." Her voice took on a dreamy quality, painting a picture of this adventurous alter-ego.

"I'd be a tech mogul, making waves in Silicon Valley with some revolutionary app," said Jenna.

Sophia's contemplative vibe lingered as she gazed into her glass. "I'm so jealous of Maggie. She actually did pick a new book from her library, didn't she? Moved away to chase a new dream."

"I wonder if she found what she was looking for, if her new life lives up to her expectations," I mused. Jenna's eyes met mine, reflecting a sense of loss, before she plastered on a fake smile.

The room fell into a thoughtful silence as we all considered the what-ifs of our own lives.

Our discussion of *The Midnight Library* wandered through themes of choice, regret, and the winding paths of destiny. Though I'll admit, my focus had started to fray somewhere between "alternate realities" and "existential longing." Because I had my own subplot brewing. And it involved a very real kiss.

Sure enough, Sophia clocked the shift in my attention. She shifted in her seat, eyes sparkling with barely contained curiosity. "Clara," she said, leaning in like a cat who knew exactly where the cream was kept, "speaking of choices and destiny… are you going to tell us more about that *very* extended lunch date at The Ivy Nook? Three hours, wasn't it? That's quite the 'not-a-date.'"

All eyes turned to me. I could already feel the blush rising. "It wasn't a date," I saidtoo quickly. "I was just showing him around."

Jenna, already grinning, raised her wine glass. "Is that what we're calling it now? Because I also heard about a certain moment in the town square that involved a kiss—and I quote—'like something out of a Hallmark movie.'"

I groaned, burying my face in my hands. "I knew the grapevine in this town was ruthless, but this is next-level."

Sophia leaned in. "Come on, spill. We've been patient. And frankly, we live for this."

I peeked out between my fingers, trying and failing to keep the smile off my face. "Fine. But for the record, that first kiss was purely scientific."

Jenna snorted into her glass. "Scientific."

"An experiment." I took a sip of my wine. Perhaps tea would have been more appropriate at this juncture, given I was about to spill some about mine and Ethan's escapades.

Leaning in closer, I adopting a tone ripe with mischief. "However, I'm lacking any scientific rationale for last night's... let's call it an 'unexpected research development."

The room exploded. Gasps, laughter, hands flying to chests like I'd dropped an entire season finale spoiler. It felt a little like high school, but in the best possible way.

Sophia clapped her hands together, her eyes sparkling. "Oh, do tell!"

Jenna leaned in, her grin spreading across her face. "Yes, spill! We're all ears. Was it a moonlit rendezvous? A spontaneous moment of passion?"

I laughed, despite the embarrassment heating my cheeks. "Okay, okay, it wasn't as dramatic as all that. We were saying goodnight, and then... he kissed me. It was soft, unexpected. Like finding a piece of a puzzle you didn't know was missing."

The women carried on, creating elaborate scenarios in which Ethan and I fall in love, get married, and run the B&B together. I refrained from telling them they'd read one too many cozy romances.

As the teasing ebbed, Eliza, pierced through the chatter, tilted her head. "Wait a minute. Back up to that 'scientific experiment' part. You can't just drop a line like that and not expect us to bite. What was that about?"

I cleared my throat. "Ah, yes," I began, choosing my words with care. "Well, it's a bit of a strange story."

Eliza and Sophia leaned in, the room going so quiet you could hear the soft crackling of the fire.

"You won't believe me." The absurdity of it all pressed in. A grown woman, seriously entertaining the idea that a sprig of mistletoe had granted her telepathic powers. What was next? Flying lessons powered by happy thoughts and candy canes?

Sophia put her hand on mine. "Come on, we'll believe you. Cross our hearts." She drew an X over her heart with her finger.

Jenna nodded encouragingly.

I looked from Sophia to Eliza, both of them practically holding their breath, eyes wide with anticipation. Sophia's curiosity I was used to, but Eliza? Eliza with her turtleneck, silver rings, and faint aura of judgment, like she curated her personality from obscure literary journals. I still wasn't sure if she was here for the book club or to write a scathing essay about it later.

Did I really want to say this in front of someone who probably thought magical realism was passé and mistletoe was for peasants?

But maybe it was the wine. Or the kiss. Or the fact that holding it in felt heavier than just letting it out.

Before I could stop myself, the words slipped free: "Whenever I kiss someone under the mistletoe, I can hear their inner thoughts."

A burst of laughter followed, led by Sophia's infectious giggle. "Clara, that's brilliant!"

But I shook my head, a small smile on my lips. "No, I'm serious. It's actually happening. The kiss with Ethan in the town square was part of that experiment."

Sophia's eyes widened. "You're not joking? You can actually hear thoughts during a mistletoe kiss?"

I recounted the tale of my mistletoe mysteries, starting with Tom, skipping Jenna, and going straight to the attempt with Ethan that mysteriously didn't work. When I reached the part about confiding in Ethan and how, instead of dismissing it as absurd, he suggested a second test at the tree lighting ceremony, all three women crooned and said how Ethan seemed like such a great catch.

Genuine interest replaced Eliza's earlier air of superiority. "That's extraordinary. But how? Is it like a sudden insight into their deepest secrets?"

I nodded. "Yes, exactly. Their fears, hopes, regrets... it's all there. But it seems to focus just on lost loves."

Sophia grinned and pointed at the mistletoe hanging in the doorway leading to the kitchen. "Why don't we test this mistletoe magic of yours right now?"

The suggestion sent a ripple of excitement through the room. Jenna's eyebrows shot up, panic settling on her features. I had omitted her from my story earlier, but maybe she was still worried I'd tell them about Maggie.

I hesitated, the reality of revealing my unusual ability in such a direct way sending a flutter of nerves through me. The idea of putting my mistletoe theory to the test in front of my friends was daunting, yet part of me was curious to see if it would work again. "Well, I suppose we could try."

"Who's going to be the test subject?" Sophia glanced around the room.

A flurry of suggestions filled the air as everyone started nominating each other, voices overlapping in a wave of giggles and excitement. The vibe that had already shifted from book club to high school now felt like a slumber party dare. Pillows, wine, and whispered challenges. Apparently, tonight's theme was *kiss the book club host and see if she's psychic.*

It would've been fun—was fun—except for the quiet swirl of doubt gathering beneath my smile. What if this whole thing *was* just in my head? What if Ethan, with all his gentle encouragement, had accidentally fueled a delusion? What if those past mistletoe moments were nothing more than well-timed flukes?

"I'm not sure," I hesitated, grappling with my thoughts. "What if it only works with that specific mistletoe, you know, the one under the old oak tree?"

Eliza waggled her eyebrows. "There's only one way to find out, isn't there?" She deftly took the wine glass from my hand, placing it on the table with a decisive clink. Then she ushered me towards the mistletoe hanging in the doorway.

I faced Eliza under the mistletoe. My heart raced, a tumultuous blend of nerves and the surrealism of the moment. Up close, Eliza's features were more pronounced—the subtle curve of her brow, the faint freckles dusting her nose, and the lightest trace of lavender on her skin, a scent that spoke of serenity amidst the storm of emotions in the room. Her eyes, a deep and thoughtful brown, held mine with an expression that wavered between playful skepticism and a hidden depth, almost as if she were daring the universe to prove her doubts wrong about my mistletoe magic.

In a bold, almost theatrical gesture, Eliza placed her hands on either side of my face, her grip gentle but assured. With a glint in her eye and the faintest lift of a brow, as if daring me to flinch, she leaned in and pressed her parted lips softly against mine.

As our lips met, the world seemed to hush. It was a stage-worthy kiss with just enough drama to make Sophia gasp and Jenna freeze mid-sip. I stilled, uncertain, bracing for awkwardness or nothing at all. Just a strange little moment to file away under *book club got weird tonight*.

But then, like a floodgate opening, the images and emotions came rushing in.

I saw a woman whose face was unmistakable: Alexandra Chase, celebrated for her unforgettable roles in cinema. Her most iconic role was as Evelyn Hart in *Eclipsed Horizons*, a film that had not only won her critical acclaim but had also left an indelible mark on the hearts of a global audience.

Suddenly, I realized I was not just a bystander in the vision; I was Eliza, experiencing each moment through her eyes. At a gala, the sensation of Alexandra's arm looped through mine felt intimate and familiar. The magnetic pull between us was undeniable, a connection that thrummed with both excitement and the forbidden. We laughed together, sharing a private joke, our combined laughter a melodic harmony amidst the event's buzz.

The scene shifted, and I was now in a living room, the ambiance intimate and private. Looking into Alexandra's eyes, I could feel the conflict and regret emanating from her. Her voice, filled with a mix of affection and apprehension, reached my ears. "Eliza, I cherish what we have, more than I can put into words. But you know how precarious my position is in the public eye. This... us... it's becoming too risky."

Feeling a surge of emotion, I found myself responding with a conviction that was deeply Eliza's. "What we have is real. Can't we find a way?"

As Alexandra reached out, her fingers brushing against my cheek with a tenderness that sent a shiver through me, her next words were laden with a painful inevitability. "You know I want to, more than anything. But my career, the life I've built, it's everything to me. I'm sorry."

The weight of her words, the finality of the moment, settled heavily in the room around us, a devastating endnote to a love that had blossomed in the shadows.

As the vision faded, and I was brought back to Jenna's living room, I exhaled, trying to process the glimpse into Eliza's past. The room was silent, all eyes on me.

Eliza and a movie star? This had to be my imagination running wild.

Disappointment tugged at me. If these visions were just figments of my imagination, then Harold's lost love was a fictional tale, and my investigation with Ethan... well, it was based on a fantasy. The thought brought a sense of regret, not just for the wild goose chase but for the missed opportunities to spend more time with Ethan under the guise of our mistletoe mystery.

Turning to face the group, I forced a wry smile, preparing to downplay the entire episode. "Well, unless my newfound 'talent' involves revealing scandalous love affairs between our book club members and celebrities, I think it's safe to say it's not very reliable."

Jenna and Sophia let out a burst of laughter. "Next, you'll be telling us Sophia's secretly dating a rock star!" said Jenna with a chuckle.

Sophia threw her hands up theatrically. "You got me, I'm totally dating the lead singer of The Midnight Echoes. We're eloping next week!"

Their laughter was contagious, and for a moment, the room was filled with a sense of light-heartedness, a welcome relief from the intensity of the vision.

But then, I noticed Eliza. She wasn't laughing. Instead, she sat there, a solemn look on her face, her eyes reflecting a depth of emotion that made my heart sink on her behalf. The laughter faded as Jenna and Sophia also turned to look at Eliza, their expressions shifting from amusement to shock.

"Eliza, you didn't actually...?" Jenna's voice trailed off.

"Clara, who did you see?" Eliza's voice was steady, but there was an undercurrent of vulnerability in her question.

"Alexandra Chase," I said, the name feeling surreal as it left my lips.

A collective gasp echoed around the room, but it was Eliza's reaction that held my attention. She took a deep breath, her eyes closing as if to brace herself. When she opened them again, there was a resignation in her gaze. "It's true. Alex and I... It was years ago, but your vision... it was true."

I sat there, processing.

A wave of astonishment swept over Sophia's face as she stared at me, her eyes wide. "This... this is real? Your mistletoe magic actually works?" She looked like someone who had just witnessed a magician pull a rabbit out of a hat.

"I can't believe it," said Eliza, almost to herself. "It's actually real."

Sophia let out a low whistle. "Clara, you're like a walking, talking lie detector test, but for love secrets!"

Jenna, on the other hand, was feigning a look of surprise, her acting skills not quite as polished. "Wow, that's... that's incredible." Her tone lacked the genuine shock of Sophia's.

"Oh, come on, Jenna, don't look so doubtful," said Sophia, misreading Jenna's tone. "You should give it a try. Let's see what Clara can uncover for you."

Jenna quickly shook her head, her expression firm. "No, no, I'm good. Really," she insisted, trying to brush off Sophia's suggestion with a casual wave of her hand.

But Sophia pressed on. "Come on, it could be fun!"

Jenna's resolve began to crumble under Sophia's enthusiastic badgering. Finally, with a dramatic sigh, Jenna threw up her arms in exasperation. "Alright, fine! I already know it works, okay? And I already know what Clara would see. I don't want to talk about it." She gathered the empty wine bottles and stormed to the kitchen.

"Oh, I... I didn't mean to..." Sophia's voice trailed off. She got up to follow Jenna. But before she could move further, Eliza reached out, stopping her with a touch on her arm.

"Let her be for now," said Eliza. "Sometimes, it's harder to share these things than we think. I should know, after all."

Sophia hesitated. She glanced toward the kitchen, then back at Eliza, and finally, with a sigh, she sat back down.

I turned my attention to Eliza, whose own confession earlier in the evening seemed to weigh heavily on her. "Eliza, are you okay?" I asked.

This had to be the most intense book club she'd ever been to.

Eliza shrugged. "Yeah, I'm okay. Just a lot to process, you know?"

I nodded. The evening had left us all a bit off-kilter. Looking to lighten the mood, I half-joked, "I wish I had one of those magic green books right about now. I'd pick one that takes us back about thirty minutes, to before we all dove into our personal soap operas."

"Perhaps we should call it a night," said Eliza.

Sophia cast a lingering look towards the kitchen, a hint of reluctance in her eyes. After a moment, she turned back to us and nodded slowly. "Yeah, that's probably for the best."

As Sophia and Eliza gathered their things, Jenna emerged, her eyes red and puffy. Sophia approached her with gentle steps. "Jenna, we're going to head out."

Eliza added a quiet, "Take care, okay?"

Jenna pulled Sophia into a tight hug.

I lingered for a moment, feeling a pang of guilt as I watched Jenna gather the remaining snacks. "Jenna, I'm sorry if..." I started, unsure of how to express my remorse for the unintended pressure of the evening.

Jenna glanced up, then returned her focus to the task at hand, her movements meticulous. "It's not your fault," she said, her voice steady but lacking its usual warmth. She avoided making eye contact, concentrating a little too intently on the snack trays.

I stepped forward, offering to help, but Jenna held up her hand. "No, really, Clara. You should go home," she insisted, forcing a lightness into her tone that didn't quite reach her eyes. "Ethan's probably waiting for you, right? If you leave now, you'll be able to get home early and surprise him. Maybe you two can have a nice dinner or something... pick up where you left off last night."

I knew her words were meant to be encouraging, an attempt to brush off the heaviness of the night. Yet, there was an underlying sadness, a subtle indication that she was still processing her own emotions. Respecting her wish for space, I gave her a small, understanding nod and quietly made my way out, leaving Jenna alone with her thoughts and the remnants of our tumultuous book club meeting.

Driving home, I found myself unexpectedly eager to share the evening's drama with Ethan, almost glad the book club ended early. The realization that he had so quickly become a fixture in my life gave me pause. It was strange how rapidly someone could become a part of your daily routine, a confidant in your thoughts and experiences. Yet, alongside this newfound comfort, there was a pang of worry. Ethan was here only temporarily, and the thought that he would eventually return to his own life, leaving a void in mine, lingered in the back of my mind like an uninvited guest.

These thoughts were interrupted as I pulled into the driveway and noticed something unusual. A flashlight beam was dancing across the attic window, its flicker of light interrupting the house's stillness.

Someone was up there.

CHAPTER ELEVEN

A LIGHT IN THE ATTIC

My heart pounded in my chest as I nudged open the door to Fireside Manor. The sweeping beam of a flashlight from the attic had set my nerves on edge. I opened my mouth to call out Ethan's name, but the word caught in my throat. Instead, a tense silence filled the space around me. The manor, usually a haven of comforting solitude, now loomed ominously, its shadows seeming to teem with secrets.

As I stepped into the lobby, each creak of the old floorboards reverberated through the silence, alarm bells in the stillness. A sharp sound cut through the quiet, making me jump with a jolt of fear. Whirling around, heart racing, I let out a sigh of relief as my eyes settled on the grandfather clock in the corner. Its solemn chimes marked the hour, the deep, resonant tones echoing off the walls. Shaking my head, I chastised myself for the impulsive decision to buy this secluded place.

"Great choice, Clara," I muttered under my breath. "A remote B&B is perfect until it starts feeling like the set of a horror movie."

I attempted to calm my racing heart. This was my home, a sanctuary I had come to cherish. I just needed to find Ethan and laugh this off later. Then I really needed to get over myself and let him help with that marketing plan, so I would always have plenty of guests and this place would never feel quite so empty and serial killers couldn't just come in and hide in the attic.

"Ethan?" My voice echoed. The silence that greeted me was unnerving, almost tangible in its weight. I tiptoed through the foyer, my steps hesitant as I faced the other rooms shrouded in darkness.

Should I switch on all the lights, announcing my presence more loudly, or continue my cautious approach? If there was an intruder, I didn't want to give away my position.

"Get a grip," I muttered to myself, trying to brush off the creeping dread. The idea of someone breaking into my house seemed ludicrous. What was I expecting? To find Ethan bound and gagged, captured by a team of cat-burglar ninjas?

But what if Ethan really was in danger? My heart clenched at the thought of some malevolent presence silently invading my sanctuary. The possibility was too horrifying to entertain.

With a deep breath, I opted for stealth. Revealing my position could be dangerous if there truly was an intruder. My steps became more measured, my senses heightened as I prepared to face whoever was in the house.

First, I approached the sitting room. The moonlight seeped through the lace curtains, casting a spectral glow that bathed the room in an otherworldly light. Long, distorted shadows stretched across the furniture. The cozy armchairs and the ornate coffee table now resembled silent, watchful figures from a gothic tale. The familiar landscape paintings on the walls took on a haunted quality. Even the soft, plush rug, which usually invited bare feet, looked like a dark void in the ghostly illumination.

I made my way to the solarium. The glass walls, which during the day bathed the room in warm, natural light, now created a shadowy, foreboding chamber under the night sky. The moonlight cast a muted glow, turning the lush greenery into a collection of dark, twisted silhouettes. Each plant and garden chair seemed to morph into an abstract sculpture, their shapes distorted and unfamiliar. It was as if the room were holding its breath, waiting for something to happen. The eerie stillness of this transformed space made me pause, a shiver running down my spine as I scanned the room for any sign of movement.

None. But, as I approached the kitchen, I noticed the soft glow of light spilling onto the hallway floor. That was odd. Perhaps Ethan had decided on a late-night culinary expedition, or maybe the kitchen appliances had started a nocturnal rebellion.

Or whomever was in the attic had an accomplice.

Steeling myself, I moved cautiously down the hallway, past the downstairs bathroom. The door was closed. I wiped the sweat from my palms and turned the knob, half-expecting to find... what exactly? A burglar freshening up? I peeked inside, my heart thudding. The bathroom was as I had left it: towels neatly hung, and no intruders using my lavender-scented soap.

With a sigh of relief, I continued down the corridor. The house seemed to creak more than usual, as if it were groaning under the weight of my fears. Probably just the house settling.

Standing at the threshold of the open kitchen, I braced myself. This was it. The moment where I'd either find Ethan nonchalantly raiding the fridge or something more macabre. Taking a deep, steadying breath, I prepared to step in.

The kitchen was empty. My gaze drifted across the room, taking in the familiar details—the kettle on the stove, the row of spice jars lined up like little soldiers, the stack of clean dishes I had left drying on the rack. Then my eyes landed on the charcuterie board I had prepared for Ethan earlier. It sat untouched, the assortment of cheeses and meats undisturbed, the wine bottle beside it still sealed.

A knot of worry tightened in my stomach. He hadn't even eaten while I was gone? That wasn't like Ethan; in the short time I'd known him, he'd never passed up an opportunity to indulge in a good snack.

The house was thoroughly quiet, with no sounds of movement or activity. Except for whomever was searching the attic with a flashlight. There was definitely someone up there. I entertained the hope that I had imagined it, but deep down, I knew better. This thorough, albeit reluctant, exploration of the downstairs was nothing more than a stall tactic.

It was time to check the attic. I grabbed my rolling pin off the counter, its familiar weight a small comfort, and headed towards the staircase. Gripping the rolling pin like a lifeline, I tiptoed up to the second floor, where the guest bedrooms were situated. The silence wrapped around me like a blanket. The only sound was the thud of my heart.

Reaching the second floor, I paused. Ethan's room was just down the hall. I moved towards it, my hand hesitating on the door. I rapped quietly, ears straining for any sign of movement inside. "Ethan?" I whispered.

Nothing. No sound of movement, no voice calling out in response. Just the oppressive silence that seemed to press down on me.

I cursed under my breath. In my panic, I'd forgotten to grab the master keys from the safe downstairs. Without them, I had no way of quietly checking the rooms. I leaned against the wall for a moment, berating myself for the oversight.

Then, as I glanced up the staircase leading to the third floor, I noticed the door to my master suite stood ajar. I always made sure that door was firmly closed and locked. I took my privacy seriously.

Tentatively, I ascended the stairs. Reaching the third floor, I peered into the sitting room that preceded my bedroom. The familiar comfort of my personal space greeted me. It looked just as I had left it—a bit cluttered, lived-in, but untouched by any intruder. My bedroom also appeared undisturbed. Clothes I hadn't bothered to pick up were still on the floor, books were strewn about on the nightstand. It was a comforting mess. Usually.

My relief at seeing my personal space untouched was short-lived, however, as my gaze fixed on the next open door—the one leading to the attic.

I stood for a moment, gathering my courage. The attic, my last place to check, felt like the most daunting part of the house. The rolling pin felt heavier in my hand. Taking a deep breath to steady my nerves, I turned towards the attic stairs. It was time to face whatever was waiting in the shadows above.

I nudged the attic door the rest of the way open and walked up the steps, my hand gripping the rolling pin tightly. My eyes scanned the dimly lit space, and then I saw the silhouette of a man rummaging through an old trunk. My heart leaped into my throat. "Who's there?"

The figure froze, then turned, shining a flashlight directly into my eyes. Temporarily blinded and driven by instinct, I lunged forward, swinging the rolling pin with the might of a woman half-convinced she was starring in her own horror film.

"Clara, it's me!" Ethan's voice pierced the panic just as the rolling pin cut through the air.

Recognition hit a split second too late. The rolling pin narrowly missed Ethan as he ducked, the flashlight clattering to the floor and casting us into semi-darkness. "Ethan?"

The silhouette of him there, amidst the shadows and secrets, eerily mirrored a moment from my past, and the haunting echo of a previous betrayal that now whispered through the dusty rafters of the attic. My mind began to drift back to my second lost love.

The day had been meant for celebration. Brian, an artist, had a way of painting my world in hues I never knew existed. Our paths had crossed through mutual friends, and our connection was undeniable. Within a year, we were inseparable, sharing a small apartment. We were serious, deeply entwined, and the future we dreamed of was within reach, now that I had secured a fantastic promotion. It was a significant step for me, one that we were both thrilled about.

Or so I had thought.

I had taken off work early, buzzing with excitement, ready for whatever magical, romantic celebration Brian had devised for us. He had a way of transforming even a simple dinner at home into an artistically crafted experience, complete with candlelight and a playlist that seemed to narrate our personal love story. His gestures, always grand and often impulsive, brought a sense of unpredictability to our relationship.

At the time, I reveled in the excitement of it all, oblivious to the undercurrents of his restlessness. Brian had a habit of disappearing for weeks, embarking on what he called 'art outings'—solitary retreats where he claimed to seek inspiration. At the time, I saw these absences as part of his artistic process, a necessary sacrifice for his passion.

Back then, I mistook his flamboyance for commitment, his wanderlust for passion. I was blind to the signs that pointed to a love that was beautiful but fleeting. Even my parents had tried to warn me. They suspected Brian was using the stability of my support and finances as a safety net for his fanciful pursuits.

My parents' doubts had infuriated me. In my eyes, they simply didn't understand that art was a legitimate career, driven by passion and not the conventional metrics of success. I defended Brian vehemently, convinced they were unfairly judging him based on outdated perceptions of what constituted a 'real job.' It was a source of tension, my parents' pragmatism against my blinded devotion, a divide that only deepened with time.

But my parents had been right.

As I opened the door to our apartment, anticipation curdled into confusion. I found Brian in the bedroom, not waiting with a bouquet or a smile, but crouched in front of my closet. His hands were wrapped around my grandmother's old jewelry box, rifling through my things like he had every right to be there.

"Brian?" My voice wavered. The sight didn't belong to the day I'd imagined. "What are you doing?"

He jumped, guilt flashing across his face before he tried to bury it under a crooked smile. "Clara! I... I was just looking for something. A surprise."

But his eyes—wide, cornered—told the truth before he said a word.

"Gran's jewelry?" My voice barely left my throat. That cold weight of dread settled in my chest, heavy and certain.

"I was going to get it cleaned," he rushed. "Maybe use a few pieces in a sculpture for you. Something special, you know?"

The lie clung to the air, too flimsy to hold.

Then I saw the papers on his nightstand. I stepped closer, heart pounding in my ears, and picked up the top page—an acceptance letter to a prestigious art school across the country. Underneath it, a denial of financial aid. Tuition numbers circled in pen, like they'd been stared at for hours. Numbers that didn't match the reality of our budget, even with my new promotion.

And just like that, the rest snapped into focus. The jewelry. It was worth enough to cover a year.

Tears stung my eyes. My hand tightened around the letter as I looked at Brian. The man I loved, the man I thought I *knew*. "You were going to sell it."

His expression crumbled. "Clara, I... I didn't know how else to..."

But the words collapsed on themselves, unfinished. The silence between us said more.

Everything we'd planned had been nothing more than sketches in pencil. Easy to erase.

He left that day without another word. The door clicked shut behind him, soft but final, like the last stroke on a painting he never meant to finish.

I stood alone in the quiet, the locket in my palm cold and heavy. It had once belonged to a woman who believed love could outlast anything. And for a while, so had I.

Back in the attic with Ethan, the memory sat like a bruise just beneath the surface. History, it seemed, had a habit of circling back.

Chapter Twelve

Unsolved Mysteries

"What on earth are you doing up here?" I lowered the rolling pin, my heart pounding from adrenaline and the shock of nearly hitting the man I was... well, I wasn't quite sure what we were.

"I heard noises." Ethan rubbed the back of his neck. "Thought it might be a raccoon or something."

For a brief second, I nodded along with Ethan's raccoon story. But then, a realization dawned on me. "Wait a minute." I narrowed my eyes. "The door to my suite is always locked. And how did you even know the way to the attic was through my bedroom?"

"I, uh, well, the door was... sort of open." Ethan's silhouette was shadowy against the faint light. I glanced pointedly at the key sticking out of the keyhole. He wouldn't meet my eyes. At least I think he wouldn't. In the dimness of the attic, his face was unreadable. Doubt gnawed at me. Had I been so absent-minded as to leave my private suite unlocked before leaving for book club? And even if that were the case, Ethan's knowledge of the attic's access through my bedroom was unsettling. His presence here, in the most personal part of my home, felt like a violation.

The overhead light was in the center of the room, between me and Ethan. After a moment's consideration, I cautiously strolled over and pulled the cord. The room instantly became bathed in a harsh, revealing brightness. "And why were you searching around in the dark?"

He shuffled his feet, looking even more flustered. "I didn't think to turn on the light. I just grabbed the flashlight and came up."

I surveyed the chaos around us. Trunks were open, their contents spilled out haphazardly, and various items were strewn about as if someone had been searching for something. The scene before us didn't align with a simple investigation of nocturnal animal noises.

"What were you really doing up here?" I shifted the rolling pin in my hand, feeling the comfort of its weight.

This didn't make sense. None of it made sense. Not the midnight attic mission, not the mess, not the look on his face. And with everything going on—early inspectors, strange timing, a creeping fear that the bank might be preparing to revoke my loan—well... the human brain could only connect so many dots before it started drawing wild conclusions.

No. That's ridiculous. He's not—

But still, I heard myself say it.

A cynical, disbelieving laugh escaped my mouth. "I mean, charming serial killer was one thing, but... a bank spy? That's a new one on my paranoia bingo card."

Ethan blinked. "Clara, I'm not spying for the bank. Why would you even think that?"

"Oh, I don't know, maybe because you're acting like a character in a bad mystery novel," I retorted. "Sneaking around my attic, playing Nancy Drew in the dark? The bank did threaten to send someone to check on their 'investment.'" I air-quoted with my free hand, my grip tightening on the rolling pin.

He ran a hand through his hair, looking genuinely perplexed. "Clara, I promise, it's not like that. I'm just—"

"What? Auditioning for a role in 'Burglars Gone Wild'?" I cut in, unable to stop myself. "You're rummaging through my things, and I'm supposed to believe it's all a big misunderstanding?"

"Wait, back up a second." Ethan's stance visibly softened, the rigidity in his shoulders easing. His expression changed to something akin to concern. "The bank? Are they really putting that much pressure on you? How bad is it?"

His sudden shift caught me off guard. I hesitated, the rolling pin feeling heavier in my hand. "It's... well, it's not great," I found myself admitting, the words escaping like a sigh. "The bank's been hovering like a vulture eyeing a roadside snack. They've been threatening foreclosure."

Good god, this man is like a human confessional booth.

Ethan's expression grew more serious. "You said Fireside Manor was struggling, but I didn't realize it was to this extent. I thought..." He trailed off, looking genuinely troubled.

As Ethan's words hung in the air, I raised an eyebrow, my grip on the rolling pin loosening. "You thought what? That you'd find something in my attic that would save the B&B?" Or hock for his next grand adventure.

"No, it's not like that. I just... I got curious. And maybe a little carried away."

The sincerity in his voice was disarming, but my instincts were still on high alert. "Curious enough to end up here, in the most private part of my home?"

He nodded, a look of contrition on his face. "I know how it looks, and I'm sorry. I never meant to overstep or make you uncomfortable. There's more to it than just curiosity, but I need you to trust me."

Trust—a small word with such significant weight. I stood there, torn between the desire to believe him and the need to protect my haven. This B&B was my dream, my refuge. And Ethan, a man I had barely known but had started to feel a connection with, was standing at the center of a mystery that threatened to unravel it all.

I looked at Ethan, but what I saw was Brian's betrayal happening all over again. "I don't know if I can trust you." The words were heavy as they left my lips. The rolling pin, once a weapon of defense, now felt like an unnecessary burden in my hand.

Ethan nodded solemnly. "I get it. I've crossed a line, and I'm sorry for that. I'll find somewhere else to stay in town tonight." His voice was low, tinged with regret.

Leave? Really? "Or, you know, you could just stay and actually explain what you're doing here."

Ethan paused, his foot on the top step, and turned to face me. His expression was one of inner conflict, etched with a hesitance that made him seem more vulnerable. After a moment, he sighed deeply. "You said it yourself, Clara. Maybe some mysteries are best left unsolved."

Then he continued down the staircase.

A part of me wanted to chase him, to ask more questions, to understand why he was really here, and when did I ever say that? But another part of me, the part still stinging from the intrusion, remained silent. So I just stood there, alone.

The attic, with its slanted ceilings and dust motes dancing in the harsh light, felt more oppressive than I had imagined now that Ethan was gone. As a kid, I'd had recurring nightmares about attics—dark, sprawling spaces where shadows lived and breathed. And now those childish fears nipped at the edges of my consciousness.

I hated coming up here, and generally had been able to avoid it. The very idea always sent a shiver down my spine. Attics were places of secrets and unspeakable horrors. And this one, with its cobwebbed corners and creaky floorboards, felt like a page torn from my nightmares. The air was thick with the musty scent of old wood and forgotten memories. It was a smell that seemed to permeate every corner. It was the kind of smell that clung to your clothes, a mix of dust, age, and a hint of mothballs, as if the past was trying to imprint itself on you.

I shook my head, trying to dispel the creepy feeling. "Get a grip, Clara. It's just an attic." But the words did little to soothe the chill that had settled in my bones. The silence up here was too thick, like a blanket smothering all sound, making the space feel more like a tomb than part of a home.

My eyes landed on the old box Ethan had been rifling through. It looked so innocuous, yet it sat there like a Pandora's box, daring to be opened. With a deep breath, I approached. As I cautiously moved further in, every shadow seemed to stretch and twist, as if alive with malevolent energy. My hands trembled as I lifted the lid, half-expecting the ghosts of my childhood fears to jump out. Instead, I found papers, old and yellowed, whispering stories of a past I never knew.

The topmost papers were a series of ledgers, their entries meticulous and neat. Each page was a grid of names, dates, and notes written in a firm, consistent hand. At the top of each ledger, in elegant, sweeping letters, was the name Meadowbrook Retreat. The dates were from the early 1960s, a time when the world outside these walls was swirling with change, yet here, in these pages was a snapshot of something more personal, more hidden.

As I leafed through the ledgers, I noticed that all the names were of women—girls, really, judging by the birthdates next to their names. Alongside each name was a date of entry, a length of stay that varied from a few months to over a year, and a date of departure. Some entries had additional notes in the margins: "Sent to St. Mary's," "Reunited with family," "Adopted out."

My eyes caught a note next to a name: "Baby girl, healthy, 6 lbs. 3 oz." The starkness of the entry, so devoid of the emotion such a moment deserved, sent a pang through my heart.

It struck me then, a realization cold and clear. My beloved bed and breakfast, with its cozy rooms and welcoming hearth, had once been a place to hide away young women facing one of the most challenging moments of their lives.

Fireside Manor used to be Meadowbrook Retreat—a home for unwed mothers. These girls had come here in their time of need, only to leave a part of themselves behind. I thought of the tears and whispered fears that must have once permeated these walls.

I stood still for a moment, the weight of this revelation settling around me. Each room, which I had so lovingly decorated and infused with warmth, now felt haunted by the echoes of a past I hadn't known. Here, in the very place where I brewed coffee and chatted with the occasional guest, young women had grappled with a society that shunned them. Did they find temporary solace within these walls, or more of the same condemnation?

The attic, once a place of fear, now felt sacred. The weight of these stories, these lives, hung in the air around me. I wasn't just the owner of a bed and breakfast; I was the custodian of a legacy, a legacy of care and secrecy, love and loss.

As I continued to explore the contents of the box, each paper, each note, felt like a nudge from the past, urging me to understand, to empathize. I closed the ledger, a newfound curiosity blooming in my chest. There was so much I didn't know about this place, about the stories these walls had witnessed. But I was determined to learn, to honor the legacy of those who had walked these halls before me.

Why had this crucial piece of history been buried? And more importantly, how had it been affecting my business? The townspeople's avoidance of Fireside Manor started to make sense. Their polite refusals, the averted gazes when I invited them to events at the B&B... It all clicked into place. It wasn't my scones they were avoiding, but a century-old scandal. The legacy of Meadowbrook Retreat, it seemed, was more enduring than any of my marketing strategies.

And how could the realtor have omitted such a significant detail? Was it ignorance or a calculated decision to keep the B&B's past a secret? Full disclosure? More like 'full of it.' The legal side of her omission was murky, but the morality? It was as clear as my decision to never use that realtor again.

Then there was Ethan. It seemed too much of a coincidence, his sudden appearance, his interest in the attic... If he knew, why would he keep it from me?

I needed answers, and the only person who might have them was walking away—maybe already gone. Time was slipping through my fingers. Confronting Ethan felt like the only path forward. I had to know whether he was simply caught up in all this or if he was hiding something.

I marched towards Ethan's room, half-expecting dramatic background music to start playing. The impending confrontation with Ethan loomed ahead, a scene I was both dreading and, weirdly, looking forward to.

After a fruitless knock at Ethan's door, I descended to the lobby, my heart thrumming. Maybe I had lingered in the attic too long. But he was still there, his belongings neatly packed, standing as if on the verge of vanishing from my life as abruptly as he had entered it. Ethan, even in this moment of departure, looked as striking as the day I'd met him. His dark hair was still styled in that effortlessly charming way, and his sharp jawline was set in a firm line, betraying a hint of the turmoil he might be feeling. He wore that city-sleek coat, making him look out of place in the rustic charm of the lobby.

The sight of Ethan, so ready to leave, ignited a fire within me, a fierce blaze of determination to unearth the answers I deserved. Yet the fact that he hadn't left yet gave me hope. "Ethan," I said, my voice steadier than I felt. "We need to talk."

His eyes, those clear, piercing blue orbs, met mine, and for a second, I saw a swirl of emotions mirrored in them—regret, confusion, maybe a touch of fear. I didn't wait for him to respond. "I saw the ledgers in the attic. Fireside Manor... it was Meadowbrook Retreat, a home for unwed mothers. What do you know about it?"

Ethan's eyes widened, and for a moment, he looked like a deer caught in headlights. Then, he sighed, a deep, resigned breath. He set his bags down, seeming to shed the weight of his impending departure. "Can we... can we sit in the parlor? I think we need a proper conversation."

With a stiff nod, I led the way. As I flicked on the light switch, the parlor transformed from its nocturnal gothic mystery into a room bathed in warm, inviting light.

We settled into the armchairs, the room's usual tranquility doing little to ease the sense of unease that hung in the air. Leaning back, I fixed Ethan with a steady, unyielding gaze. Silence stretched between us, taut as a drawn bowstring.

"I was searching for my birth grandparents," said Ethan. "I believe they were connected to this place. I traced my father's adoption back to Meadowbrook Retreat."

The memory of our date, where he had spoken of his father's recent passing and their strained relationship, surfaced in my mind. "Did you know your father was adopted? Was he aware of his connection to this place?"

"Yes," he said. "But I didn't know he had been searching for his birth mother. I think he kept it secret, not wanting to get my hopes up. I only found out after he passed. Going through his things, I discovered papers that led me here, to Serenity Falls. I came searching for answers, trying to piece together his past."

He paused, a distant look crossing his features. "And when I found out that Meadowbrook Retreat, the very place my father was adopted from, had been transformed into Fireside Manor... it felt like fate. It seemed like the universe was guiding me to stay here, under the same roof where my father's story began."

The idea that the universe had conspired to bring Ethan to Fireside Manor stirred something deep within me. For a fleeting second, I was caught up in the romanticism of it all, the notion of destinies colliding in such a poignant and unexpected way.

But then, like a cold splash of reality, the earlier part of our conversation echoed back to me. He had so many chances to tell me, to trust me with this part of his story. My momentary captivation with the romance of his quest crumbled.

"Ethan, that's... that's a beautiful story, really, it is." The bitterness in my voice surprised even me. "But it doesn't excuse the fact that you kept this from me. You had every opportunity to tell me, to include me, yet you chose secrecy over honesty."

My words seemed to hit him, his gaze dropping to the floor, unable to meet my eyes.

But my anger was a living thing now, filling the space between us with its heat. "You thought it was better to search through my attic like a thief rather than have a straightforward conversation with me. That's not fate. That's deception." And I had made a pact with myself to never again be deceived by a man.

Ethan leaned forward, his hands clasped as if he was gathering his thoughts, or perhaps his courage. "Clara, I..." The conflict in his eyes was evident—a battle between his own intentions and the realization of how deeply his actions had hurt me. He looked as if he wanted to reach out, to bridge the gap that had formed between us, but the words seemed to fail him.

"And you know what makes this even harder to swallow?" My voice rose with each word. "I trusted you with my secret, the most bizarre, unbelievable part of my life. My... mistletoe magic," I spat out the words. "We've been working together to unravel Harold Jenkins' lost love story. I let you in, into the deepest, most personal part of my world. And you? You chose to keep me in the dark."

Ethan flinched, as if each word was a physical blow. "Clara, I'm so sorry."

The feeling of betrayal stung far too sharply for me to accept his apology. "How could you think you couldn't trust me, when I trusted you so readily?" I searched his eyes for an answer, for any sign of understanding. "Was everything just a part of your search, Ethan? Were your feelings just... just convenient?"

I could feel the walls I had carefully broken down around myself rebuilding themselves, brick by brick. The vulnerability I had allowed myself to show now felt like a foolish exposure, and the hurt of his withheld truth cut deeper than I cared to admit. I stood up, began pacing the room. He was just like Brian, keeping things from me. Sneaking around. Just like Julian, refusing to let me in.

"Remember your first night here?" asked Ethan. "When you said how awful it would be if this place had been a home for unwed mothers? I... I didn't want to upset you. I thought I could find what I needed without involving you."

"So, you decided to play detective in my attic, keep secrets, all to 'protect' me? I didn't need your protection, Ethan. I needed the truth."

He took a step towards me, his expression earnest. "I didn't want to hurt you. I thought I was doing the right thing. But I see now... I should have trusted you from the start."

His words sent a cascade of memories flooding back. That first night, his seemingly innocent questions about the history of Fireside Manor. It had all been an act—the ease with which he conversed, his interest in the B&B's past. But really, he was just fishing for information. He had already decided not to tell me, even before I made that comment about homes for unwed mothers.

I took a step back. Trust was fragile, easily broken and hard to mend. And Ethan, with his secrets and his silent judgments, had fractured something between us. "Trust... that's not something you can just piece back together."

Ethan looked like he wanted to say more, but what was there left to say?

"I need time to think," I finally said, turning away from him, from the unresolved questions hanging in the air.

Ethan nodded, his shoulders sagging. "I understand. I'll... I'll go then."

And just like that, he was gone, leaving me alone with the ghosts of Meadowbrook Retreat and the echoes of a conversation that had changed everything.

CHAPTER THIRTEEN

A COLD KNOCK OF REALITY

J enna reached over to adjust a vase of wildflowers on the table, her touch as artistically mindful as ever, bringing a bit of the outside world into my serene breakfast nook. "Clara, you can't let this eat you up."

I looked up from my half-eaten croissant, meeting Jenna's sympathetic gaze. The solarium was awash in morning glow. I was slouched in an overstuffed armchair, one leg draped over the side in a pose that would make my mother cluck her tongue in disapproval.

The night before, in a moment of vulnerability, I had called Jenna, spilling my heart out about everything that had happened with Ethan. True to form, she immediately rallied the troops. Jenna, Sophia, and even Eliza had shown up on my doorstep bright and early, armed with an array of breakfast treats and the kind of flowers that only friends who truly know you can pick. As I recounted the events, the betrayal, and my own swirling feelings of mistrust and confusion, they listened, their faces a mixture of concern and anger on my behalf.

"I was really starting to trust him..." The words caught in my throat. My history with men was a rocky one. I was naïve with Alex, thinking his derision was cool, when really it was just condescending. Brian, on the other hand, was nothing but attentive... when he was around. And after catching him trying to steal from me, I had made a promise to myself: never to trust another man again. Then Julian had come along, his charm and promises sweeping me off my feet... only to leave me for someone else the night before our wedding. And now Ethan. I was repeating the same pattern, and it felt like I was trapped in a cycle I couldn't escape.

Sophia refilled my coffee cup, her movements smooth and practiced. "Trust is a garden, Clara," she said. "It needs time and care to grow. Sure, some weeds may sprout, but don't let them overshadow the beautiful blossoms. You've been through a lot, but it's the trials that make the triumphs so sweet. Keep your heart open. You're stronger than you think."

Letting Sophia's words sink in, my gaze wandered to the window, where a particularly audacious sparrow was making a show of its acrobatics. The show-off. It was a nice distraction from my thoughts about Ethan. He was like a human turducken of mystery: an enigma, stuffed inside a riddle, all wrapped up in a conundrum. And just when you think you've reached the core, you find another layer of 'What the heck?'.

Jenna gestured wildly, as if ripping out imaginary weeds. "Ethan is a dandelion of deceit. That guy needs to be uprooted from the garden of your life, Clara. And we're not just talking a gentle pull here. We need to dig deep, get him out by the roots! Maybe even throw in some metaphorical weed killer for good measure."

Sophia and Jenna shared a high-five over the table, their laughter lightening the mood. I chuckled, despite the heaviness in my heart. This was exactly what I needed.

Eliza, who had been sitting thoughtfully, finally chimed in. "I don't know, guys," she said with a shrug. "Secrets have a way of seeming necessary in the moment."

Sophia nodded thoughtfully. "And as we all know, Eliza here is a connoisseur of the clandestine. I mean, come on, a secret fling with Alexandra Chase?"

Eliza's cheeks flushed a shade of pink, but she wore a grin of pride. "I'm never going to live that one down, am I? But you're right, we all have our secrets, don't we?" Turning to me, Eliza's eyes twinkled with a playful glint. "I mean, what about you and your mistletoe magic?"

This brought a mix of chuckles and knowing glances from around the table. I laughed along, but inside, my thoughts were adrift. The investigation I had started with Ethan—our search for Harold Jenkins' lost love—lingered in my mind. It was a secret project, ironically enough, given our current conversation about the pitfalls of keeping secrets.

"Alright, fair point," I conceded. "I guess we do all have our secrets. Some are just more... magical than others."

Looking around at my friends in the solarium, with its lush greenery casting a comforting glow, I realized something. Friendship was an impressive force, a soothing balm for the heartaches life threw our way. Ethan's departure had left a void, but in this room, surrounded by love and support, I found solace.

Maybe these women could help me with my investigation. Yet, the thought of continuing the search without Ethan brought a mix of emotions. It had felt like our thing.

"But seriously." Sophia leaned in, putting a hand on my knee. "We are with you regardless of what you decide about Ethan. Secrets can be tricky. They sometimes feel necessary, but they can also create distance between people. It's a delicate balance."

Jenna nodded. "Exactly. It's about finding that line between protecting yourself and others, and being open enough to build genuine connections."

I reflected on this past week with Ethan, the intimate moments we shared. There was a raw vulnerability in the way he confided in me about his strained relationship with his father. Ethan's attentiveness to my concerns about the Manor struck a chord deep within me, highlighting a level of understanding and connection I had never experienced with Brian.

And he had encouraged my exploration of the mistletoe magic, supporting my whimsical beliefs with a sincerity that felt almost surreal. Unlike Alex, who would've laughed me out of the room with my sprig of mistletoe in hand, Ethan supported me without a hint of mockery or disdain. This part of him, this earnest cheerleader for my quirkiest bits, it made me feel seen—like someone finally noticed the oddball in the corner. A part of me wanted to write Ethan off as another charming deceiver, but there was something genuine in his eyes that my cynical heart couldn't quite dismiss.

"You know, I do think Ethan's intentions were good," I said. "We had just met, and I was a stranger to him. It's hard to gauge how much to share in a situation like that, especially something so heavy."

Jenna tilted her head. "That's true. Early in a relationship, it's hard to know what's right to share. But his later choices...."

Sophia nodded in agreement. "Intentions matter, but so do actions. And it's the actions that leave a lasting impact."

I paced the length of the solarium, each step a bid to unravel my tangled thoughts and the weighty opinions of my friends. For some reason, their digs at Ethan, deserved or not, were starting to grate on me, like a song stuck on repeat. Time to change the subject.

"And amidst all this," I said, "there's the revelation about Fireside Manor."

Jenna set down her mug. "I'm still reeling from when you told me that last night. It's unbelievable that it was once a home for unwed mothers. I've lived in this town all my life and never knew."

Eliza stopped mid-reach for a pastry, her expression a mixture of surprise and curiosity. "That's quite a discovery. It changes the entire history of the place."

I nodded, my thoughts drifting to the old ledgers and the stories they held. "It does. And not for the better. This is what Ethan was trying to protect me from. My beautiful vision of Fireside Manor is now... complicated, knowing its legacy."

Sophia furrowed her brow, a hint of confusion in her voice. "But why is a home for unwed mothers a bad thing? That seems like it would be a good thing. A way to help women who didn't have the support network or resources to help themselves."

Eliza shook her head. "It's not that straightforward. I learned about these places in my women's studies class. They were much more common before birth control finally started becoming a thing."

She paused, gathering her thoughts. "The homes were less about support and more about hiding 'unacceptable' pregnancies. They were a place where parents could sequester their pregnant daughters, telling everyone the girl was just away visiting family. These girls were shamed and isolated from society. They often faced harsh conditions, were forced to give up their babies, never to talk about them again, and received little to no support in coping with the emotional aftermath."

Sophia's expression turned somber as she absorbed Eliza's explanation. "I had no idea. That's... that's really heartbreaking."

"Yeah," I said quietly. "It adds a layer of sadness to the history of Fireside Manor."

"But remember, Clara," said Jenna, "every place has a history. Some are just more visible than others. This doesn't have to shatter your vision; it can deepen it."

"I agree," said Sophia. "You have the chance to bring light to a part of history that's been hidden away. It's like giving a voice to those who didn't have one."

Eliza added thoughtfully, "This could be an opportunity to redefine the manor. To honor its past, yes, but also to continue building your own legacy here. This place's history is rich and complex, but so is its future."

Their words challenged the initial shock and dismay I felt. "You're right," I said, a weight beginning to lift. "Perhaps I can find a way to blend the past and the present into something meaningful."

Jenna's eyes sparkled with ideas. "You could host events, tell the stories of the women who lived here. Maybe even display some historical artifacts if you can find any."

"And a portion of the proceeds could go to charities supporting single mothers," said Sophia, her eyes alight.

Their ideas were like rays of sunlight breaking through the clouds, casting a new light on what I had initially seen as a dark revelation.

Then came the knock at the door.

I stopped pacing as the knock echoed through the solarium. A flutter of hope stirred in my chest. Maybe it was Ethan, coming to apologize. Or it could be a potential guest, looking for a place to stay. The possibilities of who could be here ignited a spark of excitement as I navigated through the familiar corridors towards the lobby.

I opened the door, letting in a gust of the frigid, frost-scented air, and found Mr. Abernathy standing on the front porch. He was the banker who had helped me secure the loan for the Manor, a sweet old man whose face seemed to be in a perpetual state of apology.

Today, it seemed, was no exception.

"Clara, I'm so sorry to disturb you like this," he began, his voice quivering as he fidgeted with his hat. "I've always admired your spirit and the passion you have for this Manor. It's why I wanted to tell you this in person."

I braced myself, the unopened bank letters in the back of my mind now screaming for attention.

A shiver passed through Mr. Abernathy's frame.

Noticing the snowflakes flurry around him, some settling on his coat, I stepped back and gestured him inside. "Please, come in out of the cold."

He hesitated for a moment, as if reluctant to bring the chill of his news into the warmth of the Manor, but then stepped inside. I closed the door behind him, shutting out the biting wind and the whirl of snowflakes that seemed to dance mockingly in the air.

As Mr. Abernathy brushed off the snow from his coat, I took a deep breath. "I know I'm behind on my payments," I began, my voice steady despite the turmoil inside. "Business has been slower than expected, and honestly, I was counting on the Christmas season to turn things around."

He looked at me, his expression a blend of sympathy and professionalism. The snowflakes clinging to his coat seemed to emphasize the cold, hard reality we were discussing.

I forced a small, hopeful smile. "But I've got some help now. A marketing expert," I added, stretching the truth just a touch. Ethan did say he was in marketing, and after everything, it seemed only fair to rope him into my narrative of salvation. "I'm confident that we can turn this situation around."

Mr. Abernathy's eyes held a glimmer of hope, but it was fringed with the frost of reality. "Clara, I truly wish things were different, but the bank has its processes. A marketing plan is not going to be enough to change their minds. Without the mortgage payments..."

We stood there for a moment in a heavy silence, the gravity of the situation settling around us like the winter frost on the window-panes.

Then, with a deep sigh, Mr. Abernathy met my gaze, his eyes reflecting a depth of genuine regret. "The bank is foreclosing on Fireside Manor," he finally said. "I wish there was another way. You've brought so much life to this old place, and it pains me to bring you this news."

I felt the color drain from my face. "Foreclosing? But... how?" My mind raced, trying to piece together this impossible puzzle.

Mr. Abernathy shuffled uncomfortably. "It seems you haven't paid your mortgage. For a while, now. We've sent letters, but there's been no response."

I was speechless, my mind drifting to the envelopes forming an accusatory pile on my desk. I had kept putting off dealing with them, naively hoping that the Christmas rush would bring in enough money to cover my overdue mortgage payments. But that Christmas rush turned out to be Ethan, that turducken of mystery, emotion, and distraction.

"But... I can fix this, right? There's got to be a way to stop the foreclosure," I stammered, desperation creeping into my voice. The thought of losing Fireside Manor, a dream that had just begun to take shape, was unbearable.

Mr. Abernathy looked pained, his sympathetic eyes meeting mine. "Clara, if it were within my power, I'd help you find a way," he said. "But once the process begins, it's a matter of legal and financial procedures."

I felt a knot tighten in my stomach. "Isn't there some sort of grace period? A way to appeal? I have plans in motion. I just need a little more time."

He sighed, the lines on his face deepening with concern. "The only immediate solution would be to catch up on the overdue payments. And even then, it's not just about the arrears. You'd need to demonstrate the ability to continue making regular payments going forward."

Catching up on five months of unpaid mortgage was like trying to climb a mountain in a snowstorm. Still, the idea sparked a flicker of resolve within me. "I'll find a way," I said, more to myself than to him. "I have to."

Mr. Abernathy nodded, his expression softening. "I'll do what I can from my end, delay the proceedings until after Christmas, but after that..." His voice trailed off, leaving the sentence hanging in the air like a cloud of breath in the cold.

As the bank rep offered a few more apologetic words and left, I closed the door, feeling as though the ground beneath me had shifted. My friends' voices filtered through from the other room, a reminder that I wasn't alone in this, even though it felt like my world was crumbling.

CHAPTER FOURTEEN

APOLOGIES AND DISCOVERIES

That next morning, I sat in the parlor, feeling like a character in one of those novels where the protagonist has a 'dark night of the soul' and wakes up in an unexpected place. Which, in my case, was curled up on the chaise, clutching my guest book like a life preserver.

Yesterday had been a marathon of misery. After Mr. Abernathy's foreboding visit, my solarium transformed into a temporary support group. We cried, ranted, and even laughed in that hysterical way you do when things seem so bleak they circle back to funny. But as the day wore on, my friends, bound by their own lives, trickled out the door with promises to return if I needed them.

Left alone in these echoing halls, my wallowing shifted into a solo performance. I wandered through the rooms, each corner a reminder of dreams hanging by a thread. I had ended up in the parlor, aimlessly flipping through my guest book, tracing the scant signatures like they were lines on a treasure map. Eventually, the emotional exhaustion took over, and I dozed off there, the guest book my unintended companion in a night filled with restless dreams.

The jingle of the door chimes snapped me back to reality. I stepped into the lobby to see Ethan tentatively peeking inside, his eyes searching for a hint of welcome. He stood there, a picture of uncertainty, and despite my annoyance, I couldn't ignore the flutter in my chest. It was infuriating, really, how he could still affect me like this.

"Ethan," I said, my voice sharper than I'd intended, betraying a mix of emotions I wasn't ready to unpack. "You do know that as a guest, you're allowed to use the front door without performing a stakeout, right?"

He stepped inside, and a sheepish grin spread across his face, softening the hard lines of our recent interactions. It was disarming, that smile, and I hated that part of me responded to it. In his hand, he clutched a folder, thick with papers, holding it almost like a shield or a peace offering. "I wasn't sure if... well."

The sight of the folder piqued my curiosity. Ethan hadn't seemed the type to carry around paperwork, at least not the kind that didn't involve mysterious family histories. He approached cautiously, the folder extended towards me.

"What's that?" I nodded towards the folder while trying to mask the intrigue in my voice with a hint of casual skepticism.

"I've got something for you." He offered me the bursting folder like it was a peace treaty. Or perhaps a really comprehensive apology.

I took it, ignoring the surge of warmth that flooded through me when my fingers brushed against his. "What is this, your secret recipe for toast?"

He smiled, a bit ruefully. "A marketing plan for Fireside Manor. Consider it an apology... and maybe a way to make up for my subterfuge."

I flipped the folder open and scanned the contents. The pages were filled with meticulous graphs, detailed strategies, and a marketing plan that was undeniably thorough. It was evident he had poured a lot of effort into this. For a fleeting moment, I was impressed—how did he get this all done in two days?

Then a wave of frustration washed over me, extinguishing that brief flicker of appreciation. The meticulousness of his work only added fuel to my ire. The pages, filled with market analyses and promotional ideas, seemed to mock me with their precision. Each chart and bullet point felt like a patronizing pat on the head, a silent reminder that he believed I needed saving, needed his guidance to navigate my own life's challenges. It was as if he thought his careful planning and strategic thinking could erase the betrayal, the lies, and most of all, his misguided notion that I was some sort of delicate flower.

"You think a few fancy graphs and strategies can just make everything better?"

Ethan looked taken aback. "I thought—"

"That's just it. You thought you had to protect me. Sneak around, keep secrets, all because you assumed I was too fragile to handle the truth. I'm not some porcelain doll, Ethan. I'm not a damsel in distress waiting to be saved by your grand gestures."

The room fell silent, the tension thick between us. I could see the regret in his eyes, but it didn't quell the storm of emotions inside me. The folder in my hand felt like a band-aid over a wound that required more than just a strategic plan to heal.

Ethan's posture deflated, the confidence draining from him as he slumped into the chair nearby. He ran a hand through his hair. For a long moment, he just stared at the floor, as if he was piecing together a puzzle in his mind.

"I..." He lifted his eyes to me, and the sadness in them just about melted me. "I see it now. This... This is the same fight I always had with my dad. He was always trying to make decisions for me, thinking he was protecting me. And here I am, doing the exact same thing to you."

I crossed my arms, waiting for him to continue.

"I thought I was helping, but I was just repeating a pattern. A pattern I hated being on the other end of. I thought I was different, but I was just... just..." His voice trailed off, lost in the weight of his realization. It was like watching someone come face to face with a mirror image they never knew existed.

"I'm sorry, Clara," he continued, his voice steadier now. "Truly sorry. Not just for the lies and the secrecy, but for treating you like you couldn't handle the truth. For thinking I knew better. I didn't have the right. I don't want to be that person, the one who takes over instead of trusts."

There was a sincerity in his words that tugged at the edges of my anger, softening it just a bit. It didn't erase everything, but it was a start. A crack in the wall I had built around myself.

I sat down across from him, the folder still in my hands, now feeling more like a bridge than a barrier. "We've both got our patterns, I guess. Our ghosts. It takes a lot to face them."

He nodded, a silent acknowledgment of the complicated road we both walked.

Ethan's gaze drifted towards the door, a resigned shadow crossing his face. "I should check out, leave you in peace. I've imposed enough."

Something in his demeanor, the way he seemed resigned to walking away from not just Fireside Manor but his own quest, tugged at my heart. He had come all this way, driven by a need to connect with a past he barely understood. And despite everything, I couldn't turn my back on that. Or on the faint spark that still flickered between us.

"Ethan, wait." The words escaped me before I could weigh them. There was a tremble in my voice, a hint of something more than just concern. "In the attic... did you find what you were looking for?"

He paused, turning back to face me. The air between us crackled, a mixture of past hurts and lingering possibilities. "No, I didn't have enough time."

His words were heavy with unfulfilled longing, and not just for his past. There was a yearning in his eyes that mirrored my own, a desire to find not just his story but perhaps a shared future. I realized then that whatever our issues, it would be unjust to send him away without letting him complete his search. How could I deny him the chance to piece together his own story?

"You should stay," I said, the decision feeling surprisingly right. The words were an invitation, not just to explore the attic, but to explore the 'what ifs' that lingered between us. "Finish what you started."

His eyes widened, a flicker of hope igniting in them. "Really? You'd let me do that after everything?"

"Yes, but this time, no sneaking around. We do this openly, honestly. Together." I needed him to understand the importance of transparency in whatever was left of our journey. But there was more to it than that. It was a step towards mending whatever fragile thread still connected us.

"Thank you, Clara," he breathed out, a genuine sense of relief evident in his voice. But there was also a softness, a tentative reaching out that went beyond gratitude. "No more secrets, I promise."

As we made our way to the attic, a space filled with dust and memories, it felt like we were stepping into a new hope. In helping Ethan find his past, maybe we were both finding a path towards healing and understanding. And who knows, maybe even a future where the past didn't dictate our steps, but rather illuminated them.

"What was your grandmother's name again?" I rubbed my tired eyes, then glanced over at Ethan. The attic was cluttered with stacks of papers archiving our exhaustive search through the musty boxes and forgotten folders.

"Elsie Mae Henderson." He was sitting cross-legged on the floor, another pile of documents in his lap.

I glanced back at the paper in my hand, then at the neat stacks around us. My eyes were crossed from all the reading, and the afternoon sun was relentlessly beating through the attic window, casting long shadows across the dusty floorboards. We'd been up here for hours, rummaging through every box, every envelope, every piece of history stored in this forgotten space.

Ethan and I had both just gone through the last paper, our movements slowing as the reality set in. Nothing. Not a single document had Elsie Mae Henderson's name on it. The disappointment was a heavy weight in the air that seemed to draw us both down.

I let out a sigh, feeling the sting of frustration and sympathy for Ethan. It was like chasing a ghost. "I'm sorry, Ethan. I really thought we'd find something."

He looked up at me. The vulnerability in his eyes made my heart ache. It was a strange feeling, this blend of empathy and an unspoken connection that had somehow grown stronger despite the circumstances.

"Yeah, me too." He gathered the papers, his movements slow and mechanical, as if he was trying to piece together his emotions along with the documents.

The silence between us was filled with unspoken words, defeat, and the faint glimmer of something more.

Ethan's quiet resignation was contagious. As we tidied the scattered papers, a sense of finality seemed to settle over us. The attic, once a place of potential revelations, now felt like a chamber of lost hopes.

"I guess that's it, then." Ethan stacked the last of the papers.

I nodded, my mind still racing, unwilling to accept defeat. "It doesn't make sense, though. There has to be something we're missing." My gaze wandered over the attic, lingering on the old trunks and boxes we had already sifted through.

Ethan and I shared a look. "Let's take a break," I said. "Get some food. Then we can search the rest of the house. Maybe try the basement."

Ethan nodded, and we descended from the attic. Stepping into my bedroom, I immediately noticed how different it felt. The room was refreshingly cool, a welcome relief from the stuffiness of the attic. Ethan, looking a bit sweaty and flushed from our hours of searching, paused by the door, his gaze briefly sweeping the room.

Suddenly, I became achingly aware of every wrinkle on my shirt and streak of dust on my face. Ethan's presence in my bedroom felt unusually close, as if the walls were drawing in, making the space more intimate.

"Well, this is my bedroom," I said, trying to sound casual.

Ethan's eyes darted around the room, landing on the small details—the unmade bed, a stack of books on the nightstand. "I, uh, never went through anything in here. Just so you know."

I raised an eyebrow, a playful smirk tugging at my lips. "So, the attic was fair game, but my bedroom was off-limits? How chivalrous of you."

The corner of his mouth lifted. "I do have some boundaries, you know."

I crossed my arms, leaning back against the bookshelf. "Boundaries, huh? I'll remember that."

Ethan stepped closer, the distance between us shrinking. "Maybe I should have explored here too. Who knows what other secrets this room holds?"

I met his advance with a playful smirk, my heart racing but my voice steady. "Trust me, the only skeletons in this closet are last season's fashion disasters."

"Well, I must say, your current 'attic chic' ensemble could start a whole new trend. Dust and mystery—it's an intriguing combination." He waggled his eyebrows suggestively. "I find it rather sexy, in an unconventional, 'exploring the unknown' kind of way."

"Well, there might be some unknowns here for you to explore." I attempted what I hoped would be a sultry drape across the bookcase, but a precariously placed novel chose that moment to tumble off, landing with a comedic thud at my feet.

"Looks like your unknowns are jumping right out at us."

We both laughed, the sound filling the room and dissolving any remaining tension. Then our eyes locked. In that instant, the world outside my bedroom faded away, the humorous interlude segueing into something deeper and more intense.

Before I fully comprehended what was happening, Ethan closed the distance between us. His hands cupped my face, the warmth of his palms sending a tingling sensation through my skin. The scent of his cologne, mixed with the mustiness of the attic, created an unexpectedly comforting aroma that enveloped us.

As he leaned in, our breath mingled, the anticipation heightening my senses. The first touch of his lips was tentative, a soft brush that teased and enticed. It was like a hesitant whisper, testing the waters before committing to the plunge. But then the kiss deepened, his lips pressing more firmly against mine, confident and searching.

The taste of him was a mixture of coffee and something uniquely Ethan—a flavor that was both new and intoxicatingly familiar. As our kiss intensified, my senses seemed to heighten, making every touch, every scent, every taste more vivid.

My hands found their way to his hair, the strands soft and dusty from our earlier exertions. Pulling him closer, I surrendered to the kiss, letting go of the lingering doubts and questions. In that moment, there was only the overwhelming sensation of being completely immersed in him. In us.

Suddenly my legs felt weak, almost giving out beneath me. Ethan's arms were quick to respond, wrapping around me in a secure embrace. I wrapped my legs around his torso, clinging to him as he pushed my weight against the wall. The solidity of his body against mine was both startling and exhilarating.

His kiss grew more fervent, and I responded with equal passion, lost in the whirlwind of sensations. In that moment, all the confusion, the frustration, and the doubts melted away, leaving behind the raw intensity of our connection. I was no longer thinking about the attic, the ledger, or the secrets of Fireside Manor. All that mattered was the here and now, the undeniable chemistry that pulsed between us.

I reached out to the bookcase behind me for support. My fingers grasped onto an ornate carving on the end of the shelf behind me. There was a faint click, almost drowned out by the pounding of my heart. The kiss broke as we both paused, a mix of surprise and curiosity in Ethan's eyes.

I looked to where my hand still rested, and to my astonishment, a section of the bookcase had shifted. It revealed a small, previously unnoticed compartment—a hidden nook that had opened with my accidental pressure against a disguised lever.

I reached into the compartment, my fingers brushing against something solid. I pulled out an old, leather-bound ledger, its cover worn and faded.

Ethan and I exchanged a look of surprise and anticipation. All thoughts of lunch—or anything else—were forgotten as we sat on my bed, the old ledger lying open between us. Its pages were filled with names and dates.

"This could change everything." Ethan looked over my shoulder while I carefully turned the aged pages.

I nudged the ledger towards him. "It's your family's history, Ethan. You should be the one to look."

He nodded, his fingers tracing the lines of text as if they were precious relics. The ledger, it turned out, was a key. Each entry contained the real name of a girl in Meadowbrook's care, paired with the alias used during her stay to protect her identity.

Ethan's eyes darted across the pages, searching for the connection to his past. Then, his hand stopped, his finger resting on an entry that seemed to make time stand still.

"It can't be..." Ethan's voice trailed off as he stared at the page.

I leaned over. The name Elsie Mae Henderson was listed, but in the column for aliases. The other name, the one for Ethan's grandmother, the woman we had been searching for, was the same woman who had been so interested in Fireside Manor.

Doris Fletcher.

The pieces of the puzzle were finally coming together.

I leaned closer, peering at the entry. "Doris... She was here all along. Her story, her past—it's been part of Fireside Manor's history from the start."

Ethan gazed at me. "We found my grandmother."

CHAPTER FIFTEEN

FAMILY TIES

The evening air was crisp as Ethan and I sat in the car parked outside Doris Fletcher's house. It was the kind of charming, old-fashioned home you'd expect to find on a postcard, with a well-tended garden and a porch swing that whispered tales of bygone years. Despite the inviting facade, the car felt more like a holding cell than a vehicle, what with Ethan being too nervous to get out and approach the door.

In the end, I had been the one to call Doris and fish for a dinner invitation. We both agreed that it would just be too weird coming from Ethan, the random stranger in town. Plus, he choked every time he picked up the phone to call her.

Doris had been delighted to have us over, and invited us to dinner that Friday.

We had spent the intervening days playing amateur detectives. Our time was filled with excitement, frustration, and unexpected moments of closeness. We had become acquainted with practically every octogenarian in town, but Harold's long-lost love remained elusive. The irony wasn't lost on me; as we repeatedly failed to uncover one love story, I was tentatively exploring the beginnings of another.

Perhaps I wasn't meant to be an amateur sleuth. Perhaps the true mistletoe magic wasn't in finding Harold's lost love, but in creating this mystery that inadvertently brought Ethan and me closer.

And as we prepared to face Doris, there was a sense of hopeful anticipation that at least *this* mystery—the mystery of Ethan's biological grandmother—had been solved, and was about to come to its fruition.

Well, *I* had a sense of hopeful anticipation. Ethan, on the other hand, was a bundle of nerves beside me, his hands fidgeting with the hem of his shirt.

"I can't believe we're actually doing this," he said.

"Hey, it's just dinner, right?" I reached out to grasp his hand, stilling his nervous movements. "A bit of roast, some awkward small talk, and a life-altering revelation. Piece of cake."

He squeezed my hand, his gaze fixed on the warmly lit windows of Doris's house. "It's not every day you tell someone you're their long-lost grandson."

The porch light flickered to life. Its glow spilled out over the flower-filled front yard. The light, dancing on the petals and leaves, painted a picture of warmth and homeliness. Yet, beneath its serene facade, for Ethan, I knew it marked a daunting gateway.

There was a shift in the curtains.

"Well," I said, "I think our time for contemplation in the car has officially expired."

Ethan gave a half-hearted nod, eyes still fixed on the house.

"Remember, I'm right here with you." I gave his hand a reassuring squeeze. "We'll take it one step at a time."

Ethan took a deep breath, a determined look crossing his features. "Let's do this."

I released his hand and picked up the bottle of wine we had brought for Doris. "Here, you give her this. It'll give your hands something to do." I handed him the bottle. "With the way you've been fidgeting, Doris will have sniffed out your entire ancestry by the time we cross her threshold."

Ethan gave a wry chuckle and accepted the bottle. "Thanks. I think."

We got out of the car, our steps synchronized as we approached Doris's front door. I could feel the anticipation buzzing between us, a shared energy that made even the simple act of ringing the doorbell feel significant.

As the door opened and Doris's familiar face appeared, I took a deep breath. Ethan clutched his wine bottle for dear life.

"Clara, Ethan, so good to see you!" Doris's voice was warm, her smile genuine. Little did she know, her world was about to change.

Doris ushered us inside, her bustling energy immediately filling the space. The aroma of a home-cooked meal wafted through the air, a tantalizing mix of herbs and something roasting in the oven that made my mouth water. As we stepped into the living room, the lively strains of polka music greeted us, the sound emanating from an old record player nestled in the corner.

Ethan's nervousness seemed to ease at the familiar tunes. "Polka-holix. They're one of my favorites. You remembered."

"Of course." Doris beamed, leading him over to a carefully curated stack of records. "And I set these aside for you."

Ethan looked genuinely touched as he browsed through the collection. "Doris, this is incredibly thoughtful, but I can't accept such a generous gift."

"Nonsense," said Doris. "These records are meant to be enjoyed, and I can't think of a better person to appreciate them than you. Besides, I have plenty more where these came from."

As Doris and Ethan bonded over the accordion-driven beats of polka, I seized the chance to survey Doris's living room. The place was a charming cross between a well-ordered botanical garden and a local history museum. An eclectic mix of Serenity Falls memorabilia lined her shelves: photos, trinkets, and what seemed like artifacts from every town event since the dawn of time. Each piece seemed to be a snapshot of Serenity Falls's history. And I was itching to examine them more closely.

"Now, you two make yourselves comfortable. Dinner will be ready in a jiffy." Doris was the epitome of a gracious host, but I could see the glint of curiosity in her eyes about why we wanted to have dinner with her in the first place. It was the same look she had whenever there was town gossip to be shared.

Ethan and I exchanged a glance. He took a deep breath, visibly steeling himself for the conversation ahead.

As soon as Doris busied herself in the kitchen, humming a cheerful tune, I veered closer to her collection. Among the myriad faces in the photographs, I spotted several familiar ones. There was Tom, caught mid-laugh behind the bakery counter, and a candid shot of folks dining at the Ivy Nook, their faces lit up by the cozy ambiance. Another photo showed Jenna waving from her art booth at a town festival, her vibrant paintings forming a colorful backdrop.

Then, to my surprise, I saw a photo of myself at last year's winter festival, grinning with a cup of hot cocoa in my hand. The realization that I was part of Doris's curated world of memories, alongside these other town staples, brought a surprised and somewhat rueful smile to my face. I suddenly felt bad about all the times I saw Doris coming and ran in the other direction.

What struck me most, though, was the absence of personal family photos amidst the town memorabilia. Perhaps Doris's busybody nature stemmed from something more than just a love for gossip. Maybe, beneath her nosy exterior and the endless stream of stories, there was a thread of loneliness, a yearning for a connection she sought through the lives of others in the town.

I glanced at Ethan, who was flipping through the albums, and felt a surge of empathy not just for him, but for Doris as well. Tonight's revelation might fill a void in Doris's heart that had perhaps been there for much longer than any of us realized.

The smell of dinner grew stronger, a comforting backdrop to the undercurrent of tension. The polka music added an almost surreal layer to the moment. It was a strange juxtaposition—the normalcy of a dinner invitation, the homely aroma of food intermingling with the cheerful, accordion-driven tunes, against the backdrop of the life-changing revelations that loomed on the horizon.

"So, Ethan," Doris called out from the kitchen, her voice carrying over the sound of clattering pots and pans, "Last time I saw you, you were knee deep in the library archives. I bet you've got some fascinating stories about our little town."

Ethan smiled, but I could see the effort behind it. "You could say that, Doris. I've learned quite a bit recently, some of it very surprising."

Doris appeared in the doorway, wiping her hands on her apron. "Oh, I do love surprises! But let's save the chit-chat for dinner. You two just relax, and we'll have a lovely evening. You'll see."

As she disappeared back into the kitchen, I leaned over to Ethan. "Ready for this?" I whispered.

He nodded, a determined glint in his eye. "As ready as I'll ever be."

Soon, Doris reappeared, her arms laden with dishes that carried the promise of a hearty, home-cooked meal. The table was set in a quaint, mismatched style that somehow felt perfectly in place in her dining room.

"Here we are," Doris announced cheerfully, placing the dishes down with pride. The aroma of pot roast mingled with fresh herbs and vegetables filled the room, making my stomach rumble in anticipation.

We gathered around the table, Ethan and I taking our seats as Doris bustled about, adding the final touches to the setting. She poured a rich, dark gravy over the roast, its savory scent intensifying the welcoming warmth of the room.

"Dig in, my dears," she encouraged, taking her own seat with a satisfied smile.

The meal commenced with a comfortable chatter, Doris regaling us with the latest town news, her eyes sparkling with the joy of sharing. Her stories were surprisingly engaging. I laughed at her witty observations and the way she mimicked the townsfolk's mannerisms.

Ethan inserted the occasional comment or question, but his eyes often met mine, seeking reassurance.

As the meal progressed, and the initial buzz of conversation mellowed into a contented lull, Ethan cleared his throat, drawing our attention. "Doris," he began, his voice steady but laden with emotion, "there's something important I need to tell you."

Doris's fork paused mid-air, a look of intrigue crossing her face. "Do tell. You know I love a good story."

I reached under the table, giving Ethan's hand a supportive squeeze. This was it. The moment of truth. My heart pounded with a mixture of anxiety and excitement for what was about to unfold.

Ethan took a deep breath, his grip on my hand tightening. "My visit to Serenity Falls wasn't just out of historical curiosity. I've been searching for my biological family, tracing back my roots."

Doris's expression shifted from curiosity to cautious. "Oh? That sounds like quite the journey."

"You're a crucial part of that journey." He gulped. "I've discovered that you're my grandmother. My father was your son, born during your time at Meadowbrook Retreat. As Elsie Mae Henderson."

Ethan's words hung in the air for a moment before they registered with Doris. Her eyes were glossy with tears. "Elsie Mae Henderson," she whispered. "I haven't heard that name in over sixty years."

A myriad of emotions flickered across her face—confusion, disbelief, and then a dawning realization.

"My son," she said, more to herself than to us, as if the words were pieces of a puzzle she was putting together. "Oh, my... How is he? I was told he was adopted after... after I left Meadowbrook."

"He was adopted by a wonderful couple who raised him as their own," said Ethan. "And he lived a good life."

The hopeful gaze on Doris's face dimmed as she absorbed the weight of his words. "Lived," she repeated softly, her voice trailing off, laden with a mother's grief for the son she never knew. "When did he pass?"

"Last month."

A profound sorrow swept over Doris's face. "Last month. So recently."

"After he passed, I found papers while sorting through his things," said Ethan. "He was in the process of searching for you. I think he wanted to understand his beginnings. But he never got the chance."

"I wish he had found me," Doris whispered, her voice breaking. "I wish I had known."

She turned towards Ethan, her eyes softening. "But now," she said, a fragile smile forming through her tears, "now, I have you, my grandson. A piece of him."

"Yes, you have me." Ethan reached out, taking her hand in his. "I think my father would have been happy to know that we found each other."

"Wait here. I have something to show you." With a newfound energy, Doris left the room, leaving Ethan and me in a moment of quiet reflection.

As the sound of Doris's footsteps faded, Ethan turned to me, his eyes reflecting a whirlwind of emotions. Without a word, he reached out, and I instinctively moved closer. Our hands found each other, intertwining.

Ethan gave my hand a gentle squeeze. "Thank you," he murmured. "For being here, for... everything."

I squeezed back, offering a small, reassuring smile. "We're in this together."

A few minutes later, Doris returned, clutching a small, worn black-and-white photograph. She handed it to Ethan with a hand that trembled. "This is me holding your father. I named him James. Did he... did he get to keep his name?"

Ethan took the photograph, his eyes soaking up the faces captured in time. A warm smile touched his lips. "Yes, he did."

"Oh, thank goodness." Doris sniffed, collecting herself. "It was the one small kindness they allowed me at Meadowbrook. To hold my son, just for a moment, and give him a name before they took him away. I never knew if it was just a gesture to placate me."

Her gaze lingered on the photograph, lost in the moment it captured. "There was a nurse there, with a soft spot in her heart. She snapped this photo for me, so I'd have something to remember him by. I've treasured it all these years, always wondering. Always hoping."

Curious, I leaned in to see the photo Ethan was holding. A young Doris—she couldn't have been more than sixteen—radiant yet tinged with sadness, cradling a small baby in her arms. Her expression captured the heartache of a young mother about to part with her child.

Those curls. The same button nose. My breath caught in my throat as I recognized the young woman in the photograph. It was the girl from Harold's memory, his lost love.

"Ethan, this is her," I whispered as I pointed to the photograph of a young Doris. "This is the girl from Harold Jenkins's memory. Your grandmother was Harold's lost love."

Ethan looked from the photograph to me, a mixture of astonishment and understanding dawning in his eyes. We had given up on finding Harold's lost love. And yet here she was. My mistletoe mystery and the mystery of Ethan's grandparents had converged. It was like fate.

Doris gasped. "How on earth did you find out? I never told a soul about Harold, and as far as I knew, neither did he."

I had no idea how to answer that, but luckily I didn't have to. Ethan stepped in. "Doris, if you don't mind me asking, what happened between you and Harold? How did two people so clearly in love end up apart?"

Doris sighed, a wistful look crossing her face as she gazed into the distance, her mind traveling back in time. "It was a different era. I was only sixteen, and head over heels. But Harold was from the wrong side of the tracks. My family would never have approved. So we had to keep our relationship a secret. That was no longer an option when I got pregnant."

Ethan and I exchanged a look, the irony of our avoidance of Doris now painfully clear. In our attempts to keep our investigation under wraps, we had unwittingly bypassed the very person who held the key to the entire mystery.

She continued, her voice tinged with the pain of old memories. "When my parents found out, they insisted I tell them who the father was. They wanted us to marry—that is, until they found out who I'd be marrying. Then they decided to send me to Meadow-brook, far away from my love, to have the baby in secret."

A shadow of regret passed over her face. "They forced me to write Harold a letter, saying I never wanted to see him again, that I could never marry him. That I had met someone else, had been seeing someone else the entire time I was with him." Doris shudders. "It was cruel, but I had no choice. In that letter, though, I tried to leave hints, hoping Harold would read between the lines, understand that I didn't mean a word of it."

She paused, collecting her thoughts. "But when I came back, hoping to reconnect, I found out Harold was gone. After his mother died, he joined the army and left."

Doris sighed. "He must have believed every word of that letter. My heart broke that day, and we never got the chance to clear the misunderstanding."

Ethan's eyes were full of compassion. "That's heartbreaking."

"I am so sorry," I added, feeling the weight of their missed opportunities and unspoken words.

Doris nodded, her eyes misty. "Life is full of 'what ifs,' my dear. But we learn to live with them, make the best of what we have."

Ethan hesitated for a moment before asking the question that lingered in the air. "But Doris, what about now? Why didn't you two connect when Harold returned?"

Doris let out a deep breath, her eyes reflecting a mix of regret and resignation. "When Harold came back about twenty years ago, so much time had already passed."

Ethan reached over and put his hand over Doris's.

She looked down at their clasped hands. "I always held a flicker of hope that maybe we'd find our way back to each other. But Harold... he never reached out, never acknowledged me. He had clearly moved on. We had only been children at the time, after all. That brief romance we shared all those years ago was just a distant memory for him."

"But are you sure, Doris?" In my mind's eye, I saw again the young girl in Harold's memory, bathed in moonlight, her laughter a melody in the night. Those stolen moments they shared, full of tender affection and hidden from the world, were imprinted with a profound longing. The ache of unsaid words from Harold's heart had enveloped me during that brief connection. And then, the letter—a tangible piece of his unspoken love and dreams for a future that never came to be.

My heart ached at the thought. The memory had felt so vivid, so full of emotion. It was hard to reconcile that intensity with the idea that Harold had simply moved on and forgotten. "You know, it's not too late. You could still reach out to him."

Doris's voice was tinged with sadness. "It's painful to hold on to a love that seems to exist only in your own heart. Why reopen old wounds? I've worked so hard to forget him."

Then, turning to me, Doris's expression changed. "I guess this means you've unearthed Fireside Manor's secret history?"

I nodded solemnly. "Yes, we found old documents in the attic. It's been a revelation."

As I spoke, I noticed a shift in Doris's demeanor. It dawned on me then; though she had never set a foot inside, Doris always kept a distant yet watchful eye on the B&B. Perhaps she hadn't put it as far behind her as she claimed.

Doris let out a sigh, a trace of regret in her voice. "I'm sorry to hear that. It's a bit of a dark spot in our town's history. I'm sorry no one ever told you about it. Sometimes people just prefer to forget."

Ethan spoke up. "But the past, however painful, should never be forgotten. It's a part of who we are, and sometimes, understanding it can help us move forward."

Doris nodded. "I suppose you're right. We may not always like what we find in our history, but facing it can sometimes bring a sense of closure, or even healing."

As the evening wound down, the atmosphere softened. Ethan and Doris made plans to meet for lunch the next day, hoping to reconnect and perhaps bridge the gap of years with new memories.

"And I'll be seeing you both at the polka party, right?" Doris added with a hint of her usual spiritedness.

We exchanged heartfelt goodbyes at her doorstep, with Ethan carefully balancing a stack of polka records under his arm—now a tangible connection to his newfound family history.

Later, on the drive home, the car hummed quietly as we navigated the dark, winding roads back to the Manor. I broke the comfortable silence. "Harold Jenkins, the town curmudgeon, is actually your grandfather. That's something to wrap your head around." I glanced at him playfully. "You've clearly inherited the polka gene from your grandmother. Should I start checking for signs of curmudgeonly inheritance in you?"

Ethan chuckled, a light-hearted spark in his eyes. "I sure hope not. But imagine that—the town curmudgeon and the town busybody. What a pair they'd make!"

I laughed in agreement. "Looks like we have another grandparent reveal to deliver. This time to Harold." I paused. "But we can't just spring this on him, not without Doris's permission. Her secret is the bigger one here. Harold doesn't even know he had a son, and now a grandson."

Ethan's expression turned serious. "You're right. We need to approach this carefully. Doris and Harold have to be in the same room, to talk, to understand each other's stories."

"The polka party," I said. "We need to somehow get Harold there too, without revealing too much. It could be the perfect place for them to reconnect."

Ethan nodded, his expression turning thoughtful. "Yeah, a casual setting might be just what they need. Less pressure. We can be there to support them, but it'll give them the space to talk."

"Agreed. It needs to be their moment, their decision to share what's been left unsaid for so long. We can set the stage, but the rest is up to them."

"The challenge will be getting Harold to agree to come," said Ethan. "But with a bit of persuasion and maybe a hint of mystery, we might just pique his curiosity enough."

The plan felt like a step towards mending a decades-old rift, a chance to rewrite a small part of the town's history. And for the rest of the drive home under the starlit sky, I mused over the fact that I was actually looking forward to a polka party.

Chapter Sixteen

BINGO

I stood alone in the foyer of Fireside Manor, the old clock on the wall marking the passage of time with its ticks. Ethan was at his lunch with Doris, and I was dying to know how it went. They had invited me to join them, but something inside me suggested it would be best for them to have this time alone. A chance for some quality grandma-grandson bonding, free from any outside influences. I wanted them to establish a connection without my presence possibly steering their conversations or interactions.

As I paced the lobby, I wondered about the dynamics between them. How had they interacted? Had they found common ground, or were there awkward silences? The thought of them getting to know each other, sharing stories and perhaps uncovering shared interests, brought a smile to my face. But what if their meeting hadn't gone as hoped? What if, despite the blood relation, the generational and experiential gaps proved too wide?

This lunch was a big deal for Ethan. Finding out you have a grandmother you never knew existed isn't exactly an everyday occurrence, and I hoped Doris had offered the kind of familial warmth he might have been missing. Hopefully, she didn't overwhelm him with tales of every neighborhood cat's lineage and the intricacies of the local gardening club's latest feud.

And then there was the chance she might have turned her well-meaning, yet somewhat invasive, curiosity towards Ethan's life. Doris was a treasure, but she could turn a simple 'how are you' into an unintentional deep dive into your personal history before you'd even had a chance to pass the salt.

Lost in thought, I barely noticed the sound of the front door until Ethan and Doris stepped into the room. They were a picture of shared happiness, radiating a warmth that only comes from deep, genuine joy. And then, my eyes fell on their attire—matching Christmas sweaters.

The sweaters were a vibrant splash of color, dotted with cheerful polka dots that danced across the fabric. Doris, ever the embodiment of festive spirit, wore hers with a panache that lit up the room, the bright hues complementing her lively personality. Ethan, typically more reserved in his fashion choices, sported his with an unexpected ease, the snug fit adding an unexpectedly charming twist to his usually classic style.

"Doris insisted we get into the holiday spirit with these." A playful grin spread across Ethan's face.

I smiled back. "I can see that. You both look... very spirited."

Doris's eyes lit up with delight. "Polka dots," she said, gesturing towards the pattern on their sweaters. "Get it? *Polka* dots!"

Something about Ethan was oddly alluring in his slightly-too-small festive sweater, the fabric hugging him in just the right way. It was a look that, under any other circumstances, might have seemed out of place, but on him, it was strangely captivating.

Ethan stepped into the room with a bright yet measured look in his eyes, pausing for a moment as if weighing each word before it left his lips. "Doris came up with an interesting idea." His voice was laced with a tempered enthusiasm. "What if we host the polka party right here at Fireside Manor?

Doris beamed at me. "Oh, Clara, it's such a fun idea! And guess what? I already ran it by the Old Polksters. They absolutely love it!"

"Of course, the final call is yours." His eyes searched mine. "And just to be clear, this was all Doris' brainchild."

It was evident from his cautious delivery and the careful placement of his words that Ethan was consciously striving to respect my agency in the matter, a shift that didn't go unnoticed by me. He was coming to me with the idea, not presenting an entire party plan in a binder. My heart swelled with hope. He had taken my words into account, though I could tell from the sparkle in his eye that he wanted to have the party here.

Doris nodded enthusiastically. "It could be wonderful for Fireside, Clara. It would bring in people from neighboring towns—potential guests for your B&B. You know, polka is very popular around here. I know I can get people to come."

Ethan placed a hand on Doris's shoulder. "But it's completely your choice, Clara. We don't want to pressure you into it. It's important that you're comfortable with the idea."

Doris, catching the cue from Ethan, tried to adopt a more solemn expression. "Of course, dear. It's entirely up to you. No pressure at all." Her attempt at solemnity was endearing, almost comical, as her enthusiasm for the idea bubbled just beneath the surface.

But a polka party at Fireside Manor? The thought was intriguing. And daunting. I pondered the proposition. Doris was right—hosting a polka party could breathe new life into Fireside Manor, not just as a B&B, but as a community hub. It was an opportunity to create new memories in a place steeped in so much history, both known and unknown.

The potential of new guests, the buzz of the community, the lively music filling the halls of the Manor, was an appealing prospect. But it was also a step into the unknown, a leap into a world I hadn't fully explored yet.

As the conversation about the polka party simmered with possibilities, Doris's demeanor shifted. Her eyes held a depth of emotion, a mix of resolve and the remnants of past pain. "You know," she began, her voice soft and tentative, "I've never actually seen Fireside Manor up close. I think... I think I'm ready to face it now, to see all the changes you've made. May I have a tour?"

"Of course. Let me show you around," I said. My heart tugged. It was clear this was a significant step for her, an act of confronting memories long tucked away.

As Doris took the lead, our tour through Fireside Manor became a journey through time. In the grand living room, she paused, her gaze sweeping over the elegant furnishings. "We used to have our weekly gatherings here. Despite our circumstances, we gals filled this room with laughter and chatter." She touched the mantelpiece, tracing the intricate carvings as if reconnecting with an old friend.

The library was our next stop, its walls lined with books old and new. Doris's eyes lit up with recognition as her fingers grazed the spines of the books. "I spent countless afternoons here, lost in stories. It was an escape, a world away from the world, right within these walls."

As we moved to the dining room, Doris recalled the simple yet meaningful meals shared around the large table. "Despite everything, there was a sense of camaraderie here," she reflected. "We found support in each other, in shared experiences."

The tour took us to the sunlit solarium next. The array of plants and flowers seemed to captivate Doris. "This was a place of peace," she murmured, looking out at the flourishing greenery. "A reminder that beauty and growth could still exist amidst our struggles."

As we reached the upper floor, a hush fell over us. The corridor, lined with doors to various rooms, seemed to hold its breath. Doris's steps slowed, her demeanor turning more subdued and reflective. She stopped in front of a particular door, her hand lingering in the air.

"This was my room," she said. "This is where I had James... and where they took him away."

I asked, "Would you like to see inside?"

Doris's eyes met mine, a world of unspoken emotions swirling within them, and she managed a small, affirmative nod.

I dug out my key. With a click, the lock yielded, and the door swung open, revealing the room that had been a significant part of Doris's past.

As Doris stepped inside, the room seemed to embrace her, enveloping her in memories of joy, pain, and life-changing moments. "This is where they took him away."

Ethan, who had been a silent pillar of support throughout the tour, placed a hand on Doris's shoulder. His presence offered a quiet comfort, a recognition of the profound emotions Doris was revisiting in this room.

After a few moments, Doris said, "I'm ready to go now."

Together, we walked back through the halls of Fireside Manor, the weight of history lifting with each step. As we descended the staircase, Doris's demeanor began to shift, a lightness returning as the proximity to the room lessened.

Once we reached the lobby, Doris turned to me, a look of gratitude in her eyes. "Thank you, Clara. This means a lot," she said. "I had forgotten that not all my memories of this place are bad. Among the difficulties, there were moments of kinship, laughter with the other girls who shared my journey here."

Her gaze drifted, settling on a distant point as if she could see through the years. "Ethan helped me see that last night." She wrapped her arm around Ethan's waist and squeezed. "The past, as challenging as it may be, shouldn't be buried. It's a part of who we are. Facing it, embracing even its most painful aspects, can lead to healing, to closure."

Her words resonated with me. It was then that inspiration struck. "I'll host the polka party here. On one condition." I paused, ensuring I had their full attention. "We openly acknowledge Fireside Manor's history during the event. We find a way to honor the plights of the girls who came through these doors, to be respectful of the history that occurred within these walls, rather than bury it."

Doris took my hand and patted it. "That's a wonderful idea. Honoring the past while celebrating the present."

"It's a beautiful gesture," said Ethan.

As the tour concluded, I felt a renewed connection to Fireside Manor, not just as its caretaker but as a part of its evolving story.

The following day, Ethan and I stepped into the bustling community center for Bingo Night, a cherished local tradition and a weekly highlight for many. Including, most notably, one Mr. Harold Jenkins. And equally notably, an event which Doris was not a regular at. This was our chance to talk to Harold.

As we entered, we were immediately enveloped in the festive ambiance of the place. The large hall was decked out in even more vibrant Christmas decorations than the last time we were here; strings of twinkling lights crisscrossed the ceiling, casting a cheerful glow over the room. Garlands adorned with red and gold ornaments draped along the walls, and the towering Christmas tree still stood in the corner, its lights winking merrily at the lively crowd.

The tables were arranged in neat rows, each covered with green and red tablecloths. Bingo cards and markers were laid out, awaiting the eager participants who filled the room with a buzz of excitement and anticipation. The scent of fresh pine filled the air, along with the underlying aroma of coffee and holiday treats from the small refreshment stand Tom had set up in the back.

As we made our way through the crowd, the sound of laughter and friendly chatter surrounded us. Our eyes scanned the room, taking in the familiar faces of Serenity Falls residents, all gathered here for an evening of fun and friendly competition. It was a heart-warming sight, the community coming together in the spirit of the season, united by the simple pleasure of Bingo night.

I spotted Ms. Hattie, a vibrant presence, surrounded by a group of silver-haired ladies, all deeply engaged in an animated conversation.

Ethan nudged me and gestured towards her. "Look, there's Ms. Hattie. Should we go say hello?"

"Absolutely," I said.

We made our way over to her group. As we approached, Ms. Hattie looked up and caught sight of us, her face lighting up with a bright smile. "Clara, Ethan! So lovely to see you both here!"

"We wouldn't miss it for the world," I said, returning her smile.

One of the ladies in the group, with a playful twinkle in her eye, chimed in, "Ms. Hattie was just telling us about the upcoming polka party at Fireside Manor!"

"Yes, I'm excited about it," Ms. Hattie beamed. "It's going to be a night to remember!"

The group around her nodded in agreement, their faces reflecting a shared anticipation for the event.

"We're looking forward to it too," I said.

After a few more exchanges of pleasantries and shared laughter, we excused ourselves to continue our mission for the evening, feeling energized by Ms. Hattie's infectious joy.

Ethan and I navigated through the crowd, doing our best to appear nonchalant as we sought Harold. We discreetly searched the tables, trying not to draw attention to our purposeful movements. We must have looked like a pair of amateur spies on a covert operation, tiptoeing around in plain sight.

"It feels a bit like we're in a low-budget spy movie, doesn't it?" I whispered to Ethan.

He grinned back, nodding in agreement. "If this whole thing doesn't work out, we might have a future in espionage."

"Over there." Ethan nodded subtly towards a table near the back where Harold Jenkins was sitting, absorbed in his bingo cards. Even from a distance, Harold's presence was noticeable. He had a stoic, almost stern demeanor, his eyes sharp and focused under furrowed brows. His gray hair was neatly combed back, and he wore a simple, well-worn sweater that spoke of a man who valued comfort over style.

I followed Ethan's gaze, spotting Harold amidst the crowd. "Bingo."

We casually approached the table, feigning nonchalance as we took the two vacant chairs across from Harold. He didn't even glance up as we settled in, his concentration fixed on the numbers being called. Settling in at Harold's table felt like a small victory in our clandestine mission.

The bingo caller's voice filled the hall with a rhythmic cadence, creating a backdrop of sound that buzzed with the collective energy and anticipation of the players. As we began to dab at our cards, I stole a glance at Harold. He played with a methodical precision, his movements deliberate and practiced. It was clear he was comfortable and in his element amidst the familiar routine of the game.

The challenge now was to engage him in conversation without disrupting the focused atmosphere. The stakes felt surprisingly high for bingo.

Ethan cleared his throat. "Evening, Harold," he greeted, his voice carefully neutral. I could sense a tension in Ethan. The weight of this unacknowledged relationship with Harold was a silent yet potent presence.

Harold glanced up briefly, offering a curt nod in response. "Evening."

A mix of emotions playing across Ethan's face—a turbulent blend of longing, apprehension, and a deep, unspoken yearning—and my heart went out to him.

Seizing a moment of quiet in the game, I turned towards Harold, feigning an offhand interest. "Harold, have you heard about the big polka event at Fireside Manor?"

He adjusted his cards, searching for a B9.

"Doris will be there," I said.

Harold's hand paused over his card, a flicker of something crossing his face before he masked it with his usual stoic expression. "Polka event, huh?" he murmured, noncommittally. "Never much been one for dancing."

Just then, Edna, ever the spark of energy, leaned in from across the table. "Oh, Harold, don't be such a grump!" she teased. "You should go to the party. It'll be good for you."

Harold merely responded with a noncommittal grumble, his expression unreadable. Ethan and I exchanged a glance. More work was needed to persuade Harold. Each call of "Bingo!" was a reminder of the community spirit we hoped to capture at the party—a spirit we hoped would ultimately draw Harold in and reconnect him with his past, and more importantly, with Doris.

As the bingo game continued, Edna turned towards us. "You know," she said, "Doris told me about her visit to Fireside Manor. She said it meant a great deal to her, facing those old memories."

Ethan and I listened intently. Edna's eyes held a warmth as she continued, "And she mentioned what you're planning, Clara—honoring the Manor's history at the polka party. I think that's wonderful. It's a brave thing, acknowledging all facets of the past like that."

There was a pause as she seemed to contemplate her next words. "I must admit, I may have been a bit hasty in avoiding the place before. But it's important, isn't it? To remember."

Hearing Edna's acknowledgement and the shift in her perspective was deeply heartening. It felt like a small yet significant validation of our efforts.

"Thank you," I said. "Hearing that means a lot to me. I just hope I can do justice to their experiences."

Ethan reached over, giving my hand a reassuring squeeze.

As we focused back on our bingo cards, my phone buzzed in my pocket, an unexpected interruption. I glanced at the screen to see an incoming call from an unfamiliar number.

"Excuse me for a moment." I stepped away to answer the call. "Hello, Fireside Manor, Clara speaking."

The voice on the other end was eager. "Hi, I'd like to reserve a room for the night of the polka party."

I felt a surge of surprise and delight. "Of course, let me check the availability." I opened my online reservation app. My heart lifted. Fireside Manor was filling up fast for the night of the polka party. Reservations were coming in, some even extending their stay to multiple nights. It was more than I had dared to hope for.

After confirming the reservation and ending the call, I returned to the table, a bright smile on my face. "You won't believe this," I said, barely containing my excitement. "Fireside Manor is filling up."

Ethan's eyes lit up. "That's incredible, Clara!"

Edna clapped her hands together, beaming. "See? I told you it was a wonderful idea."

As our joy bubbled over, I noticed Harold had paused his game to listen. He looked up, a hint of curiosity breaking through his usual stoic demeanor. "Sounds like a big event you're putting together," he commented gruffly, an undertone of interest in his voice.

Encouraged, I smiled at him. "We'd love to have you join us."

Harold's gaze lingered on me for a moment, a thoughtful expression crossing his face. Then he grumbled, almost to himself, "Don't drive much at night anymore."

Seizing the opportunity, I offered a solution. "If transportation is a concern, we could arrange for someone to drive you. You could even stay at the Manor for the night. We still have a few rooms available."

He seemed to mull over my suggestion, his gaze shifting back to his bingo cards. "Might consider it," he muttered, his tone still noncommittal but less dismissive than before.

I exchanged a hopeful look with Ethan. Though Harold hadn't given a definite yes, his response was more open than we'd anticipated. It felt like we had made a small breakthrough. We just had to wait and see if the seed we planted would take root.

CHAPTER SEVENTEEN

POLKAHOLICS

After another week full of planning and preparation, the polka party at Fireside Manor was finally underway. The main hall buzzed with an energy and vibrancy it hadn't seen in years—or possibly ever.

Ethan wrapped an arm around my shoulders. "Clara, everything looks absolutely incredible! These ledgers here," he gestured towards the carefully arranged display, "they're like living pieces of history."

I followed his gaze. The display was a tasteful homage to the building's storied past as Meadowbrook Retreat. It featured ledgers, aged photos, and various memorabilia. But what I was most proud of was that I was able to put together an informative and evocative exhibit that still preserved the anonymity of the women. The ledgers, worn yet well-preserved, contained only pseudonyms. The photos, carefully selected, portrayed the retreat's day-to-day life without ever showing the faces of the women who sought refuge there.

"I'm glad it's finally all come together," I said.

The Old Polksters band finished setting up, and soon their energetic tunes filled the air. Guests streamed in, gazing in wonder at the decorations. Just then, Eliza approached us, a glass of punch in hand.

"You two have outdone yourselves. It's like stepping into a different era."

I glanced around the decked-out halls, intertwined with nods to its past. Polka dot garlands draped the walls, and a giant Christmas tree stood in the corner, sparkling with lights and vintage decorations. Fireside Manor had never looked so splendid.

"Thanks, Eliza," I said. "The events committee really went above and beyond with the decorations."

Ms. Hattie approached, gazing around with admiration. "This is my first time here, and I must say, it's absolutely enchanting. The history on display... it's so touching to see it honored this way."

Ethan and I exchanged a pleased look. "We're glad you think so," I said. "It was important for us to bring these stories into the light."

The enchanting atmosphere immediately captivated each person as they continued to arrive. They were a colorful parade in their Christmas-themed attire, a blend of reds, greens, and twinkling accessories that complemented the Manor's cheerful ambiance. I'd never seen Fireside Manor so full.

The evening was unfolding beautifully, thanks in no small part to Eliza's efforts. While Ethan went off to restock the already-dwindling refreshments, Eliza mingled with the ease of a skilled hostess. Her sophisticated charm added an extra layer of elegance to the night.

As I stood watching the guests engage with the historical displays, Ethan sidled up beside me, his presence bringing a familiar warmth. "Look at this." He gestured towards a few folk absorbed in the old ledgers and photos. "You've turned Fireside Manor into a veritable time capsule."

I nudged him lightly with my elbow. "Well, I had a bit of help from a certain dashing burglar."

Ethan's eyes reflected the soft lights of the Manor. "Dashing, eh? But seriously, these displays... they're what led me to Doris." He gave my hand a gentle squeeze. "I have you to thank for that. For letting me come back, for helping me search. You helped piece together my family."

I felt a warm glow at his words. "It's been an adventure, hasn't it? Who knew that creepy old attic held the keys to so much history."

He leaned in closer, wrapping an arm around my waist. "You know, I always thought history was just old stories and forgotten names. But you've shown me it's alive. Personal. It's us."

We turned back to the displays, watching the guests. "And the guests are acting like they've discovered hidden treasures."

"They are treasures, Clara. And so are you."

The party was in full swing when Sophia and Jenna made their grand entrance, escorting a notably grumpy Harold between them. He was an amusing contrast to the party, dressed in a sharp suit that was at odds with his dour expression. The suit, meticulously tailored, gave him an air of distinguished elegance, but it was the polka-dot bowtie that truly caught my eye.

As they approached, Sophia and Jenna glanced my way. They gestured towards Harold with a discreet thumbs up, clearly proud of their success in bringing him to the party. Despite his grumbling demeanor, there was a hint of resignation in Harold's posture, as if he had accepted his fate for the evening.

Sophia leaned in to whisper to me as they approached. "You would not believe the effort it took to get him here."

Jenna laughed. "We practically had to kidnap him. But look, he cleans up nice, doesn't he?" She gave Harold an encouraging pat on the back.

Harold just harrumphed, though I noticed the corners of his mouth twitching as if fighting a reluctant smile. He surveyed the room, his gaze landed on Doris, animatedly conversing with a group of guests. She was donned in a flamboyant, wide-skirted dress that seemed designed for dancing, a riot of colors and patterns. The skirt swished as she moved, making her a whirlwind of color and energy. Harold adjusted his bowtie and walked in her direction. But instead of addressing Doris, he walked past toward the snack table. I let out a sigh. That was okay. The night was young.

"You guys have to see this," said Sophia, barely containing her glee. She nodded towards the dance floor.

There, amidst the swirling dancers, was Eliza, with none other than Tom. Their bodies swayed in sync to the rhythm of the polka music, their laughter mixing with the melodies. Their eyes locked frequently, smiles spreading effortlessly across their faces. Every so often, Tom would spin Eliza out and then deftly pull her back in, an action met with her delighted laughter. They seemed in their own little world.

Jenna leaned in. "Looks like there's more than just one match being made tonight, huh?"

"Seems like it," I said. Eliza was letting herself be immersed in the moment, her happiness radiating. And Tom matched her energy step for step.

As the song ended, they paused, sharing a look that spoke volumes, before joining the applause for the band. They walked off the dance floor together, still chatting and laughing.

"They're so cute together," said Jenna, a hint of wistfulness in her voice.

As Jenna and Sophia drifted away into the crowd, I found my gaze wandering towards the entrance. A certain invitation I had extended was playing at the back of my mind, sparking a blend of hope and apprehension.

I felt the comforting presence of Ethan beside me, a glass of champagne in hand. "Who are we waiting for? The mayor?"

"Actually, I invited Maggie to come tonight."

Ethan's eyebrows shot up in surprise. "Maggie? As in, Jenna's unrequited love Maggie?"

"That's the one," I said. "But relax, it's just an innocent invite. Plus, who doesn't love a good love story unfolding right before their eyes?"

Ethan glanced around at the abundant mistletoe with a knowing smirk. "Ah, so the mistletoe invasion was part of Operation Matchmaker, was it?"

"Isn't that the spirit of the season? A little bit of mystery, a dash of romance, and a whole lot of mistletoe."

Ethan's eyes sparkled with amusement. "Only you, Clara."

As the evening progressed, the Manor filled with the sounds of laughter, music, and the gentle hum of conversations. It was exactly what Ethan and I had envisioned. Sensing the right moment, I signaled to Ethan, who nodded in understanding, and then made my way to the stage.

Tapping the microphone to gain everyone's attention, I waited as the room gradually quieted down, all eyes turning towards me. "Good evening, everyone. Thank you all for joining us at Fireside Manor for this special night."

I took a moment to glance around at the faces filled with curiosity and expectation. "Tonight, we're not just celebrating with music and dance. We're also embracing an important part of this Manor's history. As many of you know, I didn't understand the full history of Fireside Manor when I first became its caretaker."

I gestured towards the displays that adorned the room. "The ledgers and memorabilia before you were once hidden away in the attic, forgotten by time. Their recent unearthing by Ethan and me has unveiled a profound history. It resonated deeply with us. These pieces contain the stories of the women who passed through these doors. Each ledger, each item, holds a narrative that deserves to be heard and honored."

The room fell into a respectful silence. My eyes found Doris in the crowd, her face shining with pride. Smiling at her, I continued, "I have come to understand the healing power of facing our past."

Doris's eyes met mine as she gave a gentle nod.

"As the caretaker of this place, I want to help right some of the past wrongs that were committed here. In that vein, I hereby extend an offer. For anyone here seeking information about adoption records from that time, please know that I am committed to helping you find those connections."

"Moreover," I continued, "I've made a decision about the future of Fireside Manor. Going forward, ten percent of our profits will be donated to the Serenity Falls Women's Health Center. It's a cause close to my heart, and I believe it's a fitting way to honor the legacy of this Manor and the women who once sought refuge here."

Murmurs of approval rippled through the crowd.

"Fireside Manor bears the weight of history, and it's our responsibility to honor that. In doing so, we can help provide closure and perhaps even healing to those who were once here. Tonight, as we celebrate, let us also remember and pay tribute to the women of Meadowbrook. To their resilience, and to their stories."

As I concluded my speech, the applause that followed was heartfelt. It was a moment of pride, not just for me, but for the entire community. We were turning a new page in the story of Fireside Manor, one that acknowledged its past while looking forward to a future of giving back and making a difference.

Stepping from the stage, I was met with smiles and congratulatory words. The night was still young, but already it felt like we had achieved something truly meaningful.

My heart still racing from the speech, I noticed a small group of elderly women gathered around the historical displays. Among them was Edna, her expression particularly contemplative as she peered at the artifacts protected under glass.

Curiosity piqued, I made my way over to them. Their whispers hushed as I approached.

"Good evening, ladies," I said. "I see the displays have caught your attention."

Edna turned to me. "Oh, Clara." She glanced at the other women beside her, who shared a knowing look. One of the women placed her hand on Edna's arm. "We were all residents of Meadowbrook, once upon a time."

As I looked at the group of elderly women, my perception shifted. For a brief moment, it was as if time peeled back. I saw them, not as they were now, but as they had been—young girls, each carrying the significance of a life growing inside them, faces etched with a blend of fear, uncertainty, and hope.

"That's a meaningful thing to share," I said. The images of their younger selves were so vivid in my mind—girls in an era much less forgiving, navigating a path fraught with judgment and hardship. I could see the vulnerability, the strength that had been demanded of them too early. It was a haunting and humbling vision.

Another woman in the group, her eyes glistening with unshed tears, added, "We would love to find out what happened to our babies."

"Of course. Let's make appointments for each of you to discuss this. We can look through the records together." It was a daunting task, but one I was committed to doing, for their sake.

But could I handle all this? Balancing the responsibilities of running a now busy Manor while also helping to reconnect mothers with their children seemed like a Herculean task.

And then there was Ethan. My heart ached at the thought of him. Soon, he'd be returning to his home in the city. The time we had spent together, unraveling the Manor's past and discovering his own family history, had created a bond that I wasn't ready to let go of. His support, his shared enthusiasm for uncovering these hidden stories, had become a part of this journey. The idea of continuing without him by my side was just about more than I could handle. Could our budding romance withstand long-distance?

As I wallowed, one of the women burst into tears, bringing me back to the moment. She stepped forward, her arms enveloping me in a heartfelt embrace. "I think about my son every day," she whispered.

She pulled back, her eyes filled with a lifetime of longing and hope. Gently, she placed a kiss on my cheek. As she did, a vision flashed before my eyes—a man in his sixties, carrying a distinct resemblance to the woman before me. Images and impressions swirled in my mind: his life with a wife, three children, moments of joy and struggle. A name echoed softly in my thoughts, a clue to his identity.

As the vision faded, I looked at the woman. The man I saw was her son. Her lost love. The connection was unmistakable.

In that moment, I finally understood the true nature of my mistletoe magic. It wasn't just about romantic matchmaking, the kind found in whimsical tales. It was deeper, more significant. I was meant to be a matchmaker, yes, but of a different sort—one who reunites lost loves of a more profound kind: families and their missing pieces, mothers and their long-lost children.

I held the woman's hands, feeling a shift within myself. The magic I had been bestowed was a gift. I vowed to myself then to use it wisely.

As we exchanged contact information and set dates for our meetings, I noticed Harold standing nearby, listening. His usual stern expression was softened by a look of deep thought.

With appointments set and a promise of exploring their histories, the women thanked me and dispersed. Then Harold stepped forward, filling the space the women had just left. His gaze lingered on the displays and the group of women who had just left, his usual stoic facade softened by a thoughtful, almost introspective expression.

He turned to me. "I'd always heard rumors about this place. Never realized how many lives it impacted."

"Yeah, it's a lot to take in." Oh, the sad irony of it all! Here was Harold, unknowingly affected by this place too, yet oblivious to the full extent of its impact on his own life. A truth that lingered just out of his reach. But that revelation wasn't mine to share.

My eyes landed on Doris. Harold followed my gaze to where she was standing, hand resting lovingly on the glass display, peering at the ledger within. The sight of Doris seemed to stir something in him. It was subtle, but in that brief instant, his face revealed a complexity of emotions. Perhaps the pieces of his past were starting to align in his mind.

Just then, Maggie stepped into the room, catching the attention of many with her gorgeous attire. Her red velvet dress was the perfect embodiment of the spirit of the evening. She wore it with confidence, her smile bright and her eyes sparkling with anticipation.

Maggie took in the scene before her, then made her way through the crowd. It was then that Jenna caught sight of her. Their eyes met across the room, and time seemed to stand still. There was an intensity in their gaze that made my own heart flutter, and I was just a bystander.

The two of them came together with a natural ease, exchanging greetings that quickly evolved into deeper conversation. Their body language spoke volumes; they leaned in close, their expressions open and engaged. I wished I could hear what they were saying!

After a few minutes of animated conversation, Jenna gestured towards a quieter side room. Maggie nodded, and together they walked off, continuing their discussion away from the bustle of the party.

I watched them go, a sense of satisfaction warming me.

Then I was busy making rounds, ensuring all our guests were enjoying the party. As I replenished the chips at the refreshment table, Ethan approached to lend a hand.

It was at that moment Doris appeared. "It's time," she said. In her eyes was a resolve born of decades of waiting and wondering.

Ethan and I exchanged a quick glance. We followed Doris as she led the way towards Harold, who was engrossed in the ledger display, lost in whatever thoughts the pages had evoked within him.

The chatter and music seemed to fade into the background. Doris paused for a brief moment before stepping forward, her gaze fixed on Harold, still studying the ledger.

"They're not our real names." Doris tilted her chin towards the ledger. "Clara didn't put out the most important book—the key to who these girls really are."

Harold's eyes met Doris's.

"That's me." She pointed at a name under the glass. "Elsie Mae Henderson."

Harold turned to face her fully, his usual stoic expression giving way to one of dawning understanding. The years seemed to fall away as they stood there, two lives intertwined by a painful past.

"Harold," Doris paused to collect herself. With tears glistening in her eyes, she gestured toward Ethan. "I'd like to introduce you to your grandson."

A multitude of emotions flickered across Harold's face—surprise, disbelief, and a dawning realization converged in his eyes as he turned to look at Ethan. For a moment, he was utterly still.

Ethan stood there, a respectful yet expectant expression on his face.

Finally, Harold found his voice, though it was barely more than a whisper. "My... grandson?" His gaze shifted back and forth between Doris and Ethan.

Doris nodded. "Yes."

Harold stepped forward, his movements hesitant. Reaching out a trembling hand, he touched Ethan's arm.

Ethan offered a small, understanding smile. Tentatively, he closed the distance between them.

For a moment, Harold seemed to hesitate. Then, as if propelled by a force greater than himself, he opened his arms and embraced Ethan. It was a hug filled with the years of missed opportunities, the sorrow of separation, and the unexpected joy of reunion.

As they stepped back from each other, Harold composed himself. "Well, I'll be..." Harold muttered, clearing his throat and straightening his polka-dot bowtie with a rough hand. "This is... something." The hint of a smile tugged at the corners of his mouth.

Ethan chuckled softly. "It's a lot to take in, I know."

"How about lunch tomorrow? I'd like to... well, I'd like to get to know my grandson." There was a slight awkwardness in Harold's manner, endearing in its sincerity.

Ethan's face lit up. "I'd like that. I'd like that a lot."

Harold nodded. But then his gaze shifted, taking on a more serious tone. "Doris, we are long overdue for a talk."

Doris met his gaze. "Yes. We certainly are."

"Why don't you two use the solarium?" I said. "It's quiet, and you'll have some privacy."

My offer was met with nods of gratitude from both Harold and Doris.

Ethan watched them go, a thoughtful expression on his face.

Eventually, the polka party began to mellow. One by one, guests bid their farewells, leaving Fireside Manor in a state of contented quiet.

Those that were staying went upstairs to their rooms. The Manor, once echoing with music and laughter, settled into a serene hush.

It was during this calm that Harold and Doris reemerged from the solarium, their faces flushed, alight with a joy that seemed to have rejuvenated them both. They approached me, hands clasped together.

"I never fully grasped the impact of this place." Harold's eyes swept over the Manor, taking in its walls that had witnessed so much. "I was on the town council for decades, and I see now more than ever that Fireside Manor deserves recognition as a historical landmark. I'm going to advocate to the historical society for that. And they have grants for properties like this, to help preserve and tell their stories."

"Thank you, Harold. That means so much." It wasn't exactly what Mr. Abernathy said I needed, but perhaps with the increase in reservations, and some sort of acknowledgment from the historical society, it would be enough to hold off the foreclosure.

"And this," Harold fished a check out of his jacket pocket and extended it to me, "is to start your nonprofit. To help reconnect the families that Meadowbrook split apart. It's time for healing and for bringing together what was once lost."

I looked at the check and resisted jumping up and down in glee. With this added funding, I could afford to get caught up on my mortgage. My eyes stung. "Thank you, Harold. This means more than you know."

Doris gave Harold a gentle nudge, prompting him to shift his feet. "Clara, um, would there happen to be any rooms available for tonight?"

A soft blush colored Doris's cheeks, and a knowing smile spread across my face. "Of course." I reached behind the reception desk to retrieve a set of keys and handed them to Harold.

As they walked away, keys in hand, I turned to Ethan. "That's it. Fireside Manor is fully booked!" The words felt like a triumphant echo in the quiet of the lobby.

As we basked in the aftermath of a successful and meaningful evening, it was clear that Fireside Manor was no longer just a bed and breakfast; it had become a cornerstone of the community, a symbol of resilience and connection. And as for me, I felt ready to embrace whatever challenges and opportunities lay ahead.

Eliza, Tom, Jenna, Maggie, and Sophia all offered to stay and help clean up. The sight of my friends, ready to lend a hand, filled me with warmth.

Surveying the room, a sense of accomplishment washed over me. The night had exceeded even my wildest expectations. Buying Fireside Manor had felt like a spontaneous decision, a leap of faith born from heartbreak. But standing here now, amidst the remnants of a night that had brought so much joy and healing, I realized it was more than that. It was fate, a calling that had led me to this very moment.

I excused myself and found Ethan in a quiet corner of the room. The soft glow of the Christmas lights enveloped us, casting a warm hue that created an intimate cocoon.

"Clara, you've changed my life in more ways than I can say." Ethan took my hand, his touch sending a warm current through me. "I've fallen for you. For your strength, your compassion, your vision. For who you are."

"I've fallen for you too," I said. "It's just... hard for me to open up. I've been burned so many times before. Trust doesn't come easy."

"I know," he said. "But you can trust me. I'm not going anywhere."

He glanced upwards. "Look."

I followed his gaze to the mistletoe hanging above us.

"Kiss me," whispered Ethan, "and see for yourself."

Drawing closer, I reached up to meet his lips. As our kiss deepened, a rush of images flooded my mind—me kissing Ethan at the Winter Festival. Me walking down the stairs in my green dress. Laughing at his jokes over lunch at the Ivy Nook. Scheming to find Harold Jenkin's lost love. Covered in dust, standing in my bedroom. Giving my speech tonight. It was all me.

As we finally parted, I realized something had shifted for me. This was the beginning of a journey based on trust, one that I was finally ready to embark on. It was time to move on. Not forget the past, but stop letting it control my present.

Ethan smiled, a genuine, heartwarming smile. "See? You're not alone in this."

"I do see. And as much as I love kissing you—which believe me, I plan on doing a lot more of—maybe we should steer clear of mistletoe in the future." I flicked the mistletoe above our heads. "It's a tad disconcerting to kiss someone and see your own face in their memories. Kind of kills the mystery, don't you think?"

Ethan wrapped me into a hug. "With you, Clara, I'm sure there will always be plenty of mystery."

EPILOGUE

MISTLETOE MAGIC LIVES ON

I opened the oven door, and a wave of warmth and spiced sweetness wrapped around me like a hug. The cookies were golden and perfect. Or, perfect enough for tonight. I slid the tray onto the cooling rack and took a moment to just stand there and breathe it all in: cinnamon, sugar, vanilla... and the sound of pans clattering as someone tried to find the serving tongs in the wrong drawer again.

"Clara!" Eliza's voice rang out like a small storm. She rushed over, arms flailing. "What are you *doing* in here? You'll have cinnamon and sugar in every seam before the night's through!"

"I heard the timer go off." I shrugged and held up a slightly misshapen cookie like Exhibit A. She wasn't wrong. My dress, all shimmer and silk, had no business being in a kitchen tonight. But still. "Oh, let it be. What's a dress without a little story of its own?"

She clicked her tongue at me, eyes full of fond exasperation as she knelt to inspect the damage. "Look at you, already collecting tales in the fabric." Her fingers fussed over the folds like a fussy aunt, brushing away invisible flour dust. "This dress should be out in the ballroom, not tag-teaming with butter and baking sheets. Aren't you supposed to be getting ready? The ceremony's starting soon."

"I know, I know." I popped the cookie in my mouth and chewed while she continued to fuss. "But you know I can't help myself. This kitchen... it's where all the best stories begin."

She gave me a look, the kind that could flatten a lesser mortal, but I just grinned back at her. Eliza had become more than just a co-worker over these past months. She was like the little sister I never knew I needed. "Business at Fireside's been so good, I barely remember what it was like before you came on full-time."

"Good thing, too," she said, standing and dusting off her knees. "Because I'm not going anywhere." She gave a final, satisfied nod at my dress. "Now get out of here! And promise me, no more baking tonight."

"Fine, fine," I said, raising both hands in surrender. "No more baking. I suppose tonight's memories should be made *out there,* not just in here." I glanced around the kitchen, the heart of so much chaos and comfort. So many late nights and early mornings. So much beginning.

"Well," Eliza said, steering me toward the back stairs with a firm hand on my shoulder, "let's make sure this memory doesn't include a flour-streaked wedding party. Go. Leave the cookies to me and Tom."

I climbed the stairs, the hum of voices and soft music from downstairs fading into quiet as I reached the second floor. Each step gave me space to breathe, to think. A year ago, I'd been elbow-deep in cookie dough, scrambling to win the town over one hopeful tray at a time. I never could've guessed those same cookies would be the spark that uncovered a decades-old love story. Or that I'd end up in the middle of one myself.

In my room, I sat at the vanity and let the quiet wrap around me like a shawl. I reached for the sprig of mistletoe I'd saved and tucked it into my hair. It wasn't the most traditional accessory, but it felt right. That tiny green bough had been the beginning of everything.

I caught my reflection in the mirror—eyes wide with nerves, mouth curled in something between a smile and a squeal. Tonight, I wasn't just hosting a celebration at Fireside Manor. I was part of its story now. A real character. And this? This was a new chapter.

I took a deep breath, adjusted the mistletoe one last time, and stepped out into the hall.

At the guest room door, I paused and knocked before poking my head inside. What I saw made my throat tighten.

Edna stood behind Doris, carefully adjusting the lace along her shoulders. The gown fit her like it had been made just for her—a beautiful vintage piece that shimmered in the golden evening light. And somehow, the room itself seemed to glow, like the house knew what was happening and decided to pour a little extra magic into the air.

I dabbed at my eyes before anything could smudge. No one needed to see the hostess with mascara running down her cheeks. Not yet, anyway.

"There you are!" Doris beamed, practically glowing with excitement. Edna tutted behind her, still adjusting the final flourishes on Doris's veil while trying to keep her from turning her head.

"You look beautiful," I said. "Are you ready?"

"Oh, my dear, I've been ready for this since I was sixteen." Doris smoothed a hand over her skirt and glanced at her reflection. "To think, after all these years, I finally get to marry my soul mate. And here, of all places."

I caught her gaze in the mirror, and in that moment, we shared something quiet and powerful. The weight of memory, the depth of what Fireside Manor had held—and now, what it had healed.

At the top of the grand staircase, I paused beside Edna, my hand resting on the polished banister. Evergreen garlands wound their way down the railing, lit with fairy lights that gave the air a golden shimmer. The deep green of our bridesmaid dresses matched the garlands perfectly, and for once, I let myself soak in the beauty of it all. I waited for my cue.

The music paused, then shifted into a lilting melody that carried warmth and joy on each note. Edna stepped forward first, graceful and poised, and I followed behind her with careful steps, my full concentration aimed at not tumbling down the stairs.

At the bottom, Ethan stood waiting, looking handsome enough to steal the air from my lungs. He offered his elbow and leaned in close, whispering, "Hello, gorgeous."

My heart did something fluttery and foolish and lovely all at once. Together, we had pieced together Doris and Harold's story. And now, we got to help usher in its happiest chapter.

Inside the living room, Harold stood tall and proud, his eyes glistening. This was their moment, surrounded by the community they'd spent a lifetime loving. Today, they were finally making their forever official.

As Ethan and I made our way down the aisle, my mind drifted—just for a heartbeat—to a future version of this walk. One where the vows were ours. But that was a thought for another day. For now, I took my place beside Edna and caught a twinkle in her eye. She wasn't looking at Doris or Harold. She was looking across the aisle at one of the groomsmen. And he was looking back at her like he'd just remembered something important.

I grinned. Love was in the air tonight, and not just for the bride and groom.

I spotted familiar faces throughout the crowd. In the front row, Jenna and Maggie sat close together, hands intertwined. Maggie had started visiting every weekend. Watching them now, it was easy to believe they'd always been together.

In the center of the room sat a woman in her eighties, her eyes bright with joy. She was surrounded by family—her son, the daughter-in-law she'd only recently met, and a small child with sticky fingers and a crooked bow in her hair. The woman had given up her baby long ago, when the world hadn't given her another choice. Now, decades later, they were here, together.

A few rows behind them sat an older man with two adult children on either side of him. Their hands rested gently on his, and their children stood nearby, watching with wide eyes and open hearts. He had lost them once, but now they were here, part of his life again.

These were the stories that made Fireside Manor more than just a place. This was the real magic—not the mistletoe, not the sparkle or the soft lights or the grand staircase, but the people. The healing. The way love kept finding its way back.

Reunited Roots had started as a fragile idea, a thread pulled from my strange little gift. Now, it was real. And it was changing lives.

The music shifted again. All eyes turned toward the back staircase as Doris made her entrance. I felt a tear slide down my cheek as I watched the town's favorite busybody walk down the aisle to marry the curmudgeon who'd secretly adored her for decades. Who would've guessed?

I thought back to the day I first arrived in Serenity Falls, weighed down by failure and doubt. But now, standing here in this room full of warmth and second chances, I knew all of it had led me exactly where I needed to be.

The ceremony passed in a blur of laughter, tears, and vows spoken through smiles. When Harold and Doris kissed, the whole room erupted into applause. I caught Ethan's eye, and the look he gave me sent a rush of warmth through my chest. No matter what came next, I knew we'd face it together.

When the noise softened and the room melted into clinking glasses and joyful chatter, I slipped away for a moment of quiet. I wandered to my favorite reading nook, tucked away behind the library shelves, where the world felt a little softer.

He laughed. "I mean, if you need someone for the holiday rush and the midnight ghost tours..."

"How could I say no to that?" I said. "You're hired. On every level."

He beamed. "So that's a yes?"

"Absolutely."

And that was it. No grand gesture. No lightning bolt. Just the soft, certain feeling of home.

As we danced beneath the twinkle lights, surrounded by friends and second chances, I held Ethan's hand and looked toward whatever came next. The manor had its magic. But the real magic was here—in the love we'd found, the people we'd helped, and the future we were building.

One kiss. One cookie. One story at a time.

GRATITUDE

I can hardly believe it. I'm actually here, launching my first novel into the world! It has been a long and windy road, and I did not make this journey alone.

A heartfelt shoutout to Isa and Keyna, my partners in literary crime these past few years. Your friendship is a treasure beyond measure, and your insights into my drafts have been transformative. Together, we are the dynamite Kick Ass Alpha team, and I couldn't have asked for better co-conspirators on this wild ride!

And to the brilliant minds at Fictionary. Oh, how my data-loving heart swooned over your software from the first click! Charts, graphs, and spreadsheets to map out my narrative? Sign me up twice! But more than that, it's the vibrant community you've nurtured that keeps pulling me back.

To my stellar beta readers, Elaine, Linda, and Janet. Your keen eyes polished this story until it gleamed. Thank you for your dedication and sharp critiques.

And to my incredible husband. Thank you for riding shotgun as I swerve down yet another new career path. Your support is my anchor in the ever-changing tides of life. Here's to new beginnings and the magic that comes from pursuing what lights your soul on fire.

CLARA'S MAGICAL SPICE COOKIES

Ingredients:

- 2 2/3 cups all-purpose flour, soft as a cloud

- 1 tsp baking soda, powdered by the breath of a dragon

- 1/2 tsp salt, harvested from the tears of joyous sea nymphs

- 1 tbsp ground cinnamon, infused with stardust

- 1 1/2 tsp ground ginger, gathered under a full moon

- 1/4 tsp ground nutmeg, from the secret groves of fairies (please ask permission before harvesting)

- 1/4 tsp ground cloves, whispered by ancient spirits

- 1 cup unsalted butter, softened, as gentle as a summer breeze

- 1 1/2 cups granulated sugar, sweet as a serenade

- 1 large egg, with the warmth of a newborn phoenix

- 1/3 cup molasses, tapped from the roots of the world tree

Instructions:

1. Preheat your oven to 350F (equivalent to the warmth of a friendly hearth) and line a spacious baking sheet with the paper of the parchments.

2. In a cauldron of medium size (or just a bowl), whisk together the flour, baking soda, salt, and spices. Set this concoction aside as you prepare to summon the magic.

3. In a grand mixing bowl, using a hand or stand mixer with the paddle attachment, blend the butter and sugars on medium-high speed. Allow them to dance together for 2-3 minutes, until they become smooth, light, and as airy as clouds in the sky.

4. With a gentle flick of your wrist, scrape down the bowl and add the egg, molasses, and vanilla extract. Continue mixing on the same speed for another 2-3 minutes, until the mixture becomes silky, light, and as creamy as moonlight.

5. Pour in half of the enchanted dry ingredients and mix on medium-low speed until they are barely combined. Then, with the grace of a woodland nymph, scrape down the bowl and add the rest of the dry ingredients. Mix again on the same low speed until just combined.

6. Use a magical rubber spatula to manually mix the dough, ensuring that every bit of magic is evenly distributed.

7. Scoop out portions of the dough and roll them into enchanted balls.

8. Place about 12 cookies on the parchment-lined baking sheet, spaced evenly apart like stars in the night sky. Bake for 13-15 minutes, or until the edges are a light golden brown and the center is pale and puffed with magic. The cookies will darken, flatten, and settle as they cool.

9. Allow the cookies to rest on the baking sheet for about 3 minutes, allowing time for the spell to complete, before transferring them to a cooling rack to cool completely.

10. Continue baking the rest of the cookies, and then gather your loved ones to enjoy the magic of these delightful treats!

BACKGROUND RESEARCH

SPOILER ALERT!

Did you skip ahead to this section before you read the book? THEN LEAVE. NOW. Unless you want spoilers, that is. Because the background research for this book ties directly to the main mystery.

In writing this story, I found myself immersed in research on the history of maternity homes. I want to share some of what I learned with you.

Maternity homes, or homes for unwed mothers, have a complex origin dating back to the early 1890s. Managed by organizations such as the Florence Crittenton Association of America, Catholic Charities, and the Salvation Army, these homes were a response to the severe social stigma against single motherhood that existed at the time. Ironically, this era also experienced an increase in premarital pregnancies and newborn adoptions. Between 1952 and 1956 alone, an estimated 1.5 million babies were placed for adoption in the United States.

The prevailing belief was that adoption served the best interests of both child and birth mother, and pressure for mothers to surrender their children was immense. As a result, many young women were sent to these homes to give birth in secrecy, only to return home as if nothing had happened. Often, staff at the homes listed these young mothers under pseudonyms, so that adopting parents did not even know the true name of the birth mother.

Maternity homes peaked in the United States during the post-World War II era, particularly in the 1950s and 1960s, and persisted until 1972. At the height of this period in the 1950s, a time known as the Baby Scoop Era, over 200 maternity homes existed across 44 states. These homes primarily housed white, middle-class teenage girls.

A significant cultural shift began in late 1960s to mid 1970s, driven by the advent of birth control, the women's liberation movement, and evolving societal attitudes towards single parenthood. The number of adoptions began to decline as support for single mothers increased, reducing the need for secretive maternity homes.

Today, the situation for unwed mothers has transformed dramatically. Modern homes, often referred to as maternity homes or residential programs, provide a range of supportive services focusing on the well-being of expectant mothers. These facilities—there are now over 400 such homes—strive to offer a safe and nurturing environment, supplemented with resources like prenatal care, educational programs, counseling, and postpartum support. Examples of such homes include:

- **Lifehouse Maternity Home** in Louisville Kentucky, providing a safe place for women and teens facing unexpected pregnancy.

- **Maggie's Place** in Arizona, which provides safe housing for homeless or solitary pregnant women, offering support with employment, healthcare, and parenting skills.

- **Good Counsel Homes** in New York and New Jersey, which takes a holistic approach by providing housing, counseling, education, and job preparation support.

- **Florence Crittenton Services**, offering comprehensive health, educational, and social services to pregnant and non-pregnant teens across several states.

- **Several Sources Shelters** in New Jersey, which provides housing along with educational guidance, prenatal care, and life skills training to foster self-sufficiency.

The Maternity Housing Coalition keeps a list of affiliated homes on their website (https://natlhousingcoalition.org/find-a-home) . These organizations embody a modern approach to supporting unwed mothers, emphasizing empowerment, education, and long-term well-being.

Despite these advancements, many single mothers continue to face significant challenges, including societal judgment, financial insecurity, and limited access to healthcare and educational opportunities.

Do you feel called to support single mothers? Consider advocating for comprehensive healthcare, childcare, and educational opportunities. You can also make a meaningful difference by donating to or volunteering with organizations that provide these essential services. By doing so, we can help ensure that every mother has the support she needs to thrive and that the stigma of the past does not dictate the future of any woman or child. Together, we can truly make a difference in the lives of many.

For further reading:

Christian, Gina. "Maternity homes offer a 'haven' that gives moms chance at 'directional change' in life." *Catholic Review.* May 13, 2023. https://catholicreview.org/maternity-homes-offer-a-have n-that-gives-moms-chance-at-directional-change-in-life/

Karnasiewicz, Sarah. "The children they gave away." *Salon.* May 11, 2006. https://www.salon.com/2006/05/11/fessler_qa/

Leventry, Amber. "'Maternity homes' still exist—then vs now." *Scary Mommy.* March 5, 2021. https://www.scarymommy.com /pregnancy/maternity-homes

Lily News, The. "A 'shame-filled prison: Inside the maternity homes that forced teen moms to give away their babies." *The Washington Post.* November 22, 2018. https://www.washingtonpost.com/gender-identity/a-shame-fille d-prison-inside-the-maternity-homes-that-forced-teen-moms-to -give-away-their-babies/

Randall, Rebecca. "For decades, churches forced unwed mothers into adoptions." *Sojourners.* October 17, 2023. https://sojo.ne t/articles/decades-churches-forced-unwed-mothers-adoptions

Riddle, Katia. "Maternity homes provide support in a post-Roe world, but not without conditions." *NPR.* May 9, 2023. https://www.npr.org/2023/05/09/1174323027/maternity-ho mes-provide-support-in-a-post-roe-world-but-not-without-con ditions

Strickland, Sheeka. "The Forgotten Home." *Medium.* March 25, 2015. https://medium.com/@sheeka_s/the-forgotten-home-5 b914565ddba

Tuinman, Gwen. "Unwed mothers and maternity home history." *Gwen Tuinman*. Undat-
ed. https://gwentuinman.com/2020/05/27/delving-deeper-un
wed-mothers-and-maternity-home-history/
Vollers, Anna Claire. "Faith-based maternity homes 'create a
haven' in states with strict abortion laws." *Stateline*. October
3, 2023. https://stateline.org/2023/10/03/faith-based-maternit
y-homes-create-a-haven-in-states-with-strict-abortion-laws/

About the Author

I'm Iris Applewood, your friendly neighborhood magical realist, cooking up worlds of wonder from my quaint home in Southern Indiana. I've always believed that the boundaries between the mundane and the magical are just waiting to be blurred. And boy howdy, do I love blurring them!

In my spare time, you'll find me tinkering in the kitchen, where I channel my creativity into concocting delightful dishes and perfumes that could almost pass for potions. When I'm not busy mixing spices or stirring tales, I cherish my sleep. It's like pressing the reset button on my imagination. Dreamland is often where I stumble upon my next big story idea, so you bet I take my bedtime seriously!

Writing is my way of stitching a little more enchantment into the fabric of our lives. And as you dive into my stories, I hope you find that magic can bloom in the most unexpected of places. Perhaps even in your own backyard.

Want to know more about me? Scan the QR code below to sign up for my newsletter. Or go to www.irisapplewood.com

FRAGRANCE OF FORGOTTEN TRUTHS

CHAPTER 1: HOMECOMING

Please enjoy this preview of the next book in Serenity Fall – A cozy mystery featuring a perfumer protagonist

I rolled down my window to get a better view as my Uber turned onto Serenity Falls' historic Main Street. The car wove past The Purple Pantry, with its purple-and-white striped awning. A few doors down, the open door of The Cozy Cup beckoned, letting the aroma of fresh coffee spill onto the street. It was a scene from a storybook. Albeit, one penned by an author with an affinity for cobblestones and an aversion to modern architecture. It was also a scene I hadn't seen in almost a year. Too long. I should have—

No. The past was the past. No sense dwelling.

"Pretty different from the city, I reckon?" Roger glanced at me through the rearview mirror. His voice carried the lilt of someone who had spent years driving these streets, narrating the town's tales to anyone who would listen.

"Oh, absolutely. Less honking, more ... honking?" I replied, as a gaggle of geese strut past The Enchanted Oven.

Roger's laughter filled the car. "That's Serenity Falls for you. Swapping traffic jams for goose parades. These birds think they own the town, and frankly, they might be right."

I didn't tell him I grew up here; my family's reputation often invited more whispers than welcomes. Anyway, surely he saw my last name when he accepted my ride request.

As we crossed through an opening in the flood wall, a panoramic view of Riverside Park spread before me, bursting with spring greenery. The cherry trees were ripe with buds, and daffodils lined the meandering paths. Whisperwind River twinkled under the afternoon sun. And there was the Whisperwind Bridge, where, legend had it, you could trade a secret for a wish. At least that's what my grandmother used to say, usually followed by a wink.

I whispered a secret there once. I was still waiting for that wish to be fulfilled.

The road wove between the flood wall and the park before transitioning into a narrow gravel lane. People seldom frequented this part of town since the construction of the flood wall. There wasn't much to see back here anymore, other than the house everyone avoided, occupied by the family everyone shunned.

"This it?" Roger slowed the car as we approached the house at the end of the road. His eyes lingered on the structure. "The Attar residence, isn't it?"

An old Victorian house loomed. The house's once-vibrant yellow paint now flaked and curled, peeling away like sunburnt skin. Despite the wear, it stood proud amidst the wild embrace of overgrown gardens and the dense Serenity Forest looming at its back.

"That's the one." I side-eyed the turret as I opened the door. It seemed to frown down at me.

After a moment's pause, Roger unbuckled his seatbelt and stepped out of the car with a friendly yet reserved demeanor. "Let me get those bags for you."

I nodded. Good. He wasn't going to say anything.

As Roger drove off, I stood before my family's ancestral home, taking it all in. The front garden had given over even more to nature's whim than when I had last seen it. Flowers tangled with creeping ivy, creating lush greenery that climbed up the walls of the house.

I'd have to do something about that.

With a deep breath that tasted like childhood, I lugged my suitcase down the stone path. My wheels clicked against the porch steps, a soft counterpoint to the birdsong overhead. I paused before the blue front door and pressed the doorbell.

After all this time away, it would feel odd to just waltz right in.

The door swung open, and there stood Emilia, auburn hair in a messy bun, wearing sweats and a t-shirt that read *Murder Shows and Comfy Clothes*. "Anna! You do exist outside of a Zoom screen!"

I stepped into the embrace of my little sister. Though at twenty-six, she was not so little anymore. "Confirmed. I'm not just a sophisticated AI after all."

Emilia pulled back, scanning me with playful scrutiny. "Well, if you were, I'd have to ask for a refund. The sister algorithm seems a bit off."

I self-consciously brushed a hand through my usually neat hair, which now felt like it had surrendered to a bout of turbulence. And I could only imagine the state of my makeup. Anyway, I had nothing to dress up for now. "Travel chic?"

Emilia laughed. "You do look like someone who's just survived a three-hour tribute to the wonders of commercial aviation. But don't worry, you're in Serenity Falls now. Here, the dress code strictly enforces comfort over couture."

She gave me a reassuring pat on the shoulder. "It's good to see you without all the city polish. I am sorry about your job, though."

"Thanks." I offered a strained smile. "Makes the city polish less necessary now."

That research job had consumed so much of my life. The long hours and missed family moments, all sacrificed at the altar of corporate ambition. I had barely even managed to escape for a few days to attend Mom's funeral last year, as it happened to overlap with a big client meeting that "only you can handle, Anna." And my repayment? A terse meeting, cold handshakes, and a severance check meant to erase years of toil and loyalty.

"Six weeks' severance for six years of everything I had," I muttered.

"Did you say something?" Emilia grabbed my suitcase out of my hand.

"No, nothing." I allowed Emilia to take the suitcase. "But what was the point of it all? I'd been with that company since graduation. Where's the appreciation?" I was teetering on the edge of a rant. With a conscious effort, I reined in my emotions.

Emilia put a hand on my arm. "It's okay. You're here now."

I swallowed my anger and stepped inside. *Whoa*. The foyer, which had once been a warm hug of family memories, greeted me now with a ... different ... ambiance. Gone were the familiar rows of family photos. These walls bore a more contemporary look, adorned with abstract art that brought a modern vibe to the space. The floral wallpaper, a hallmark of our mother's classic taste, had been replaced with gray paint.

As Emilia set my suitcase by the winding wooden staircase, I wandered into the living room. It, too, had transformed under Emilia's hand. Shelves of true crime thrillers now stood where Mom's delicate china used to be displayed. Emilia had moved Gran's armchair to face the floor-to-ceiling window overlooking Serenity Forest. It was like a different house.

"I've been making some changes," Emilia said, a note of understatement in her voice.

I felt a pang for Mom's past that once filled these walls, now giving way to Emilia's present. But it was nice to see my sister find her footing. Really, who could blame her for wanting to make the home her own now?

"It's different, I know."

Say something nice, Anna. "It's ... good." I offered what I hoped was a supportive smile. "Mom would have liked seeing it loved and lived in."

Emilia's eyes brightened. "I hope so. And Gran, she's okay with it, you know. In her own way."

She hesitated, then added, "I haven't touched Gran's suite, though. I just ..." She trailed off, shaking her head as if brushing away a thought too fragile to voice. "I keep thinking she'll come back to it, that she'll need it just as it was."

I swallowed hard. Hope was a stubborn thing.

Instead of pressing, I simply nodded.

The appearance of a plush gray cat interrupted our conversation. He leaped gracefully from the top of a bookcase that now occupied the space where our mother's cherished curio cabinet once stood. The cat wound himself around my legs.

"And this little guy showed up on my doorstep a few days ago. When I opened the door, he rushed inside and has refused to leave since. I've posted an ad on the neighborhood app, but no one seems to be missing a cat. I've decided to call him Watson."

"You named him after Sherlock's sidekick." I crouched down to give the cat a hello and a scratch behind its ears. Then I gazed up at my sister, nodding pointedly at her shirt. "So, you're still into all that true crime stuff."

"You could say that." Emilia gave a sheepish grin, motioning for me to follow her. We left the living room and navigated into the kitchen. The window over the sink bathed the room in natural light, highlighting the massive cork board that dominated the wall where mom's pots and pans used to hang. This board was cluttered, not with recipes or cooking notes, but with newspaper clippings, photos, and notes about unsolved mysteries and true crime.

"A murder board?" I raised an eyebrow. "Where did the pots and pans go? How do you even have room to cook with all this?"

"Cook? What strange magic is that?" Emilia grabbed a box of chicken crackers and a can of spray cheese and set them on the counter between us. "I DoorDash like a civilized person."

She opened the box and pulled out two crackers, then sprayed cheese in waves to cover the top of hers. She handed the cheese can to me, then gestured towards the board. "This is for the series I'm watching. I like to try to figure out the killer before the detective does."

"Of course." I carefully sprayed my cheese into a flower shape on my cracker and popped it into my mouth whole, then examined the murder board. This murder hobby couldn't possibly help my sister's reclusive tendencies.

Thirsty, I opened the fridge to get a soda. There was a distinct lack of groceries within. Finally, a problem I could solve. Grabbing a soda from the vegetable drawer, I said, "I'm not really into solving murder mysteries, but maybe I'll do some cooking while I'm here. It could be a nice change of pace. Help get my mind off things."

"I'm so glad you're here, Anna. This house has been too quiet without you."

I froze, can halfway to my lips. *She* could have come to visit *me*. In the ten years since I'd left for college, not once had Emilia made the trip. After Danny, she'd pulled the curtains tight on the world. Mom and Gran had tried to coax her back, even lined up a therapist. But Emilia dug in, even landing a remote job as an import logistics coordinator. Aside from not going out, she appeared perfectly fine. Content, even. Like she'd taken up residence in the eye of a storm no one else could see.

But I caught myself. A weight settled in my chest. "I should have come back sooner. After the funeral, and everything ... I just got caught up in my own world."

With me living so far away, Emilia had been left to shoulder the responsibility of Gran's deterioration after Mom's death. And the fact that my sister did it with no attempt to make me feel guilty about it only intensified my guilt.

Emilia reached across the kitchen table, her fingers squeezing my hand. "You're here now, and that's what matters. Let's make the most of it, right?" Her voice was encouraging, yet I could sense the underlying strength that Emilia had cultivated over the difficult months.

"Right." I nodded, making a silent promise to myself to be more present, to share the weight that my sister had been carrying alone.

I carried my suitcase upstairs into my old bedroom. What a blast from the past! Posters of my favorite bands from high school still adorned the walls. Well-thumbed novels and diaries lined my bookshelf, exactly as I had left them. Even the bedding, with its retro floral pattern, remained unchanged. The room was a monument to my teenage self.

This would have to change. Surely Emilia still had some of Mom's, or even Gran's, old stuff lying around that I could pick through to find more ... ahem ... adult decorations.

I walked over to my mirror, still bordered with photos. There I was in my science fair glory, standing proudly next to my aromatherapy study from eighth grade—charts of lavender's effects on stress levels. Beside it, Emilia and I grinned with gap-toothed smiles and ice cream-smeared cheeks, maybe nine or ten years old, our arms thrown around each other's shoulders on what must have been someone's birthday.

My eyes lingered on the sole photo of my dad. He was leaning against his old Chevy, sunlight catching in his hair the same way it sometimes did in mine, his eyes crinkling at the corners as he looked at something beyond the camera's frame. Something about his stance suggested he was already halfway gone, even then.

As I ran my fingers over a photo of my teenage self, arm draped over the shoulder of my old bestie Vee at a long-forgotten concert, a bittersweet smile formed on my lips. Despite the town's cool reception towards my family, there had been pockets of warmth and joy to be found.

My family, with our unorthodox ways and an old, enigmatic house straight out of a horror novel, had always been the subject of whispers and sidelong glances. Heck, the distinct lack of Attar men was enough to set the more old-fashioned townsfolk gossiping. Like seriously, there was no mystery there. Grandpa died of cancer, Dad ran off, and Emilia and I ... well, we just haven't found our forever people yet. But then again, our town was not known for their logic. Some have even gone so far as to blame us for a fifty-year old flood.

Us. Not bad zoning or poor infrastructure. Not the fact that the town had ignored years of warnings from actual engineers. Nope. It was the Attar women, with our herb gardens and odd hours, calling down storms like biblical plagues.

Yet, within these walls and among these photos, I could remember the good times—the laughter, the unshakable kinship that defied the town's wary glances. It was a strange kind of comfort, clinging to these memories, especially as I stood in front of the mirror now, staring at the space between past and present.

The girl in the photo, with her bright, expectant eyes, was nothing like the woman staring back at me now. My hair, once an unruly mass of auburn curls, was now straightened into submission, a misguided attempt at looking 'professional.' My features were sharper, my blue eyes carried the weight of things learned the hard way.

Was it a good change?

The realities of adulthood had tempered the carefree girl I used to be. Had I lost something in the process? The part of me that laughed too loudly, dreamed too recklessly, believed in magic without hesitation?

Nah. I'd grown up, that's all.

The city, the corporate grind, the relentless pursuit of success had sculpted me, honed me, turned me into the unstoppable force I was today.

The unemployed force.

I sighed, then heaved my suitcase onto the bed. As I placed my belongings in my old dresser, a small, dusty bottle caught my eye. I picked it up. It was my favorite perfume, a concoction Emilia and I had created under Gran's guidance. We thought this perfume was going to solve all our problems. A magical perfume to transform us into the prettiest, most popular girls in school. It hadn't worked, of course. But we wore that perfume religiously, anyway.

The label, faded but still legible, bore the name Whisperwind Whimsy.

Memories of my grandmother flooded through me, vivid and warm. We were back in the kitchen, laughter mingling with the scents of herbs and flowers.

"A dash of lavender for a calm mind, and a hint of rosemary for remembrance." Gran's hands had expertly maneuvered the array of herbs and flowers on the table. She crushed the lavender in a mortar, the fragrance intensifying with each grind. "You must treat each herb with respect; understand its nature." She poured pure alcohol over the crushed herbs. "Remember, Anna, every scent tells a story. It's not just about the fragrance; it's about the feelings it evokes, the memories it awakens."

Coming back to the present, a sigh escaped my lips. How simple life had seemed then. What I wouldn't give to go back to that time, when my grandmother was still lucid. When mom was alive. When dreams were just a scent away.

Want to read more? Order at your favorite retailer!